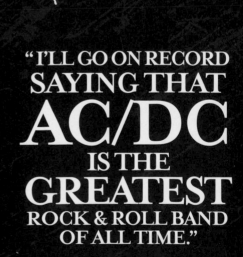

"I'LL GO ON RECORD
SAYING THAT
AC/DC
IS THE
GREATEST
ROCK & ROLL BAND
OF ALL TIME."

— RICK RUBIN

ALSO BY ANTHONY BOZZA

NONFICTION
Whatever You Say I Am

COAUTHOR OF
Slash with Slash
Too Fat to Fish with Artie Lange
Tommyland with Tommy Lee
INXS: Story to Story with INXS

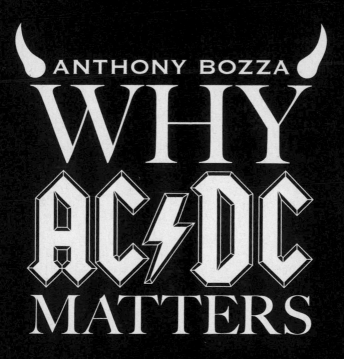

ANTHONY BOZZA

WHY AC/DC MATTERS

WM

WILLIAM MORROW

An Imprint of HarperCollins*Publishers*

HarperCollins books may be purchased for educational, business, or sales promotional use. For information please write: Special Markets Department, HarperCollins Publishers, 10 East 53rd Street, New York, NY 10022.

FIRST EDITION

Designed by Todd Gallopo @ Meat and Potatoes, Inc.

Library of Congress Cataloging-in-Publication Data has been applied for.

ISBN 978-0-06-180460-1

09 10 11 12 13 RRD 10 9 8 7 6 5 4 3 2 1

‘FOR MY WIFE, SHANE,’
who knows why they matter
more than anyone I've ever met

CONTENTS

IN THE BEGINNING

WHY AC/DC MATTERS TO ME

is much less important than why AC/DC matters to you. If I could, I'd like to know why each one of you picked up this book in the first place. I'm not just speaking to you fans, who know why you're reading these words. I'm speaking to the rest of you: the randomly curious who have opened the cover, or those of you who know someone who loves AC/DC but don't understand why they do. You're all the same to me: all of you have opened this book in search of an answer. You want to know what it is that makes AC/DC special. You want to know what it is about them that moves people—and how they do it so well.

Even if it's just for this passing moment, consider yourself hooked by what I call the greatest living rock band. To get a glimpse of AC/DC is to know them, because even a photograph of them onstage, in their element, communicates their authenticity better than a list of their achievements ever could. Statistics may explain their net worth and commercial viability, but only the experience of their live show—even secondhand—gives those statistics meaning.

Established in 1973, this Australian rock band has become the second-bestselling popular music act of all time. AC/DC has sold 200 million albums worldwide, including 71 million in the United States alone. *Back in Black* (1980) is the fifth-bestselling album in U.S. history at 22 million copies sold. That album hit number one in the UK and number four in the U.S., where it remained in the top ten for 131 weeks. The band's coheadline concert with the Rolling Stones in Toronto in 2003 holds the record for the largest paid music event in North American history, boasting attendance of half a million people. In 2005 and 2006, AC/DC landed on Australia's list of the top ten highest-earning entertainers of the year, despite the fact that they hadn't released an album since 2000 or toured since 2003. In 2008, thirty-five years after AC/DC first took to the stage, their sixteenth studio album, *Black Ice,* debuted at number one in twenty-nine countries around the world, despite the fact that it was only available in Wal-Mart and Sam's Club stores or via the band's Web site. In an era that has seen CD sales morph from a clear indication of an artist's popularity to a relic of an antiquated time, AC/DC's back catalog has continued to sell as well as it always did—or better: in 2007, in the United States alone, the band sold more than 1.3 million CDs, despite not having released a new album in six years. Since 1991, when SoundScan began tracking CD sales in the States, AC/DC has sold more than 26 million albums, outselling the Rolling Stones, the Who, Madonna, Michael Jackson, and Led Zeppelin. Today they're second only to the Beatles.

From the start, AC/DC was ridiculed by the music press. In 1976, *Rolling Stone* reviewer Billy Altman (whose writing in that magazine and elsewhere seems to indicate that he prefers covering music he doesn't like) had this to say about *High Voltage,* the band's first U.S. release: "Those concerned with the future of hard rock may take solace in knowing that with the release of the first U.S. album by these Australian grossout champions, the genre has unquestionably hit its all-time low. Things can only get better (at least I hope so) . . . AC/DC has nothing to say musically." Altman's disdain was essentially mirrored by the majority of mainstream critics until 2008, when *Black Ice* was praised across the board as a masterpiece of consistency. For the first time in twenty years, a band who'd been derided for doing just one thing was championed for doing just that. What had been called a lack of imagination for two decades was suddenly being lauded as uncompromising integrity.

Like the pioneers who transformed Australia from a prison colony to a nation, all but one of the essential members of AC/DC were born elsewhere. They were, however, raised there and imbued with the idiosyncratic cultural confluence that makes that island unusual. As it has done for Australian culture from the start, the continent's isolation has allowed for European and American traditions to be distilled, altered, and regurgitated into uniquely original permutations. AC/DC is no different: they processed rock and roll from a singular perspective and devoted themselves to it with the rough-and-tumble attitude of a pack of outsiders looking in. Their nonnegotiable distance from the core sculpted their dedication to and appreciation for jazz, blues, and rock as they evolved, on the other side of the world, into a group that has paid the greatest modern tribute to the raw roots of American rock and roll. They incorporated the influences of Chuck Berry, Jerry Lee Lewis, Muddy Waters, and Bo Diddley with those of second-generation carriers of the torch like Alvin Lee, Jimi Hendrix, John Mayall, Eric Clapton, and the Who, and brought it all together in a sound and attitude all their own. Theirs is a wild-eyed cry of unruly youths from a country founded by convicts. They mastered the basics and amplified tradition until the music overloaded, then sealed it with a simple invocation: "If you want blood—you've got it."

My first brush with AC/DC is no more important than any of yours, but I feel the need to talk about it before I say anything more. I first encountered the band when I was about ten years old. My friend up the street and I were perfectly happy tossing around *Star Wars* action figures, recreating shoot-outs with Sand People on Tattooine—until we discovered the wondrous world inside his older brother's bedroom. When we were sure that he'd gone out, we'd push open his door to peer into his sanctuary. We were never bold enough to enter, but staring in from the doorway, I was both terrified and intrigued by what I saw. There was a Pink Floyd poster (*The Wall*) featuring that iconic, silently screaming face; a Led Zeppelin poster featuring the wizardly rune symbols from the cover of *Led Zeppelin IV* and their fallen angel Swan Song logo. But front and center, in an unforgettable velvet black-light rendition, was the portrait of AC/DC that graces the cover of *Highway to Hell*. The purple light wasn't even on, but that image held me like a tractor beam, both intimidating and inviting. Young as I was, I knew it was naughty and wrong. It was a picture of the bad kids I'd heard about. Today that shot still oozes everything AC/DC stands for, the image at once charming, dangerous, rebellious, misbehaved, and tongue-in-cheek. At that point in my young life, Angus's horns and tail scared me, but for the first time, I *wanted* to be scared.

Music has always been important to me, and from the time I was about five I started paying attention to who wrote the songs I heard on the radio. I started reading credits and liner notes as soon as I was old enough to work my parents' record player, and as a teen I devoured all the writing about music I could find. I grew up in an interesting time of transition, when key aspects of society as it is today were just taking hold— from technology and the way people communicate to how and what pop culture we consume. In that period of the late '80s the old-guard music magazines lost their footing, only to convince themselves, with grunge in the '90s, that they'd regained it and were still able harbingers of musical taste and cultural moments—before ungraciously face-planting from their own shortsightedness when the industry and the times changed in the '00s. Today, for better or for worse, the most honest music reviews can be found by taking the median temperature of online forums and sifting for the truth.

Even when I was still working for *Rolling Stone,* it seemed to me that most music criticism had strayed far from what I consider the essential prerequisites of writing about music: an open-minded yet definitive point of view, an encyclopedic knowledge of the past, and a writing style that conveys, as much as possible, the experience of the music. Good, traditional music writing is of course still out there (Sasha Frere-Jones in the *New Yorker,* Alex Ross anywhere, and David Fricke never disappoint), but to me, most music reviews these days read like collegiate exercises in jaded objectivity or as experiments in mass acceptance. Too many reviews and columnists echo each other's style and opinions with no exciting writing in sight.

There is another book in that, but the way it applies to this one is simple: I'm sick of seeing AC/DC begrudgingly acknowledged. I'm sick of mainstream critics acting surprised when confronted with the band's demonstrable achievements and continuing popularity among generation after generation of obsessively devoted fans. I'm tired of the critical subtext that AC/DC is a band for the tasteless masses, that it is unworthy of the serious consideration afforded bands (like the White Stripes) mining blues and rock with calculated pretension. Don't get me wrong: there is no wrong way to mine those traditions when done well. My issue is that outside of the hard rock and metal music media, AC/DC is still seen as an inexplicably popular band that sells the obvious to an unseen, uncultured majority. That community is exactly the audience that rock snobs snub; writing for them, about their bands, has never been a mainstream priority.

To them I say this: AC/DC is the greatest living rock band, end of story. I heartily invite anyone to disagree, agree, or comment, if they care to, at my Web site, www.anthonybozza .net. There is a forum there waiting for you, and it won't take you long to make your voice heard. The Greeks believed that informed argument, discussion, and debate paved the path to knowledge, and I couldn't agree more.

I'm writing this book because it needs to be written, as much for me and for those of you who already know why AC/DC matters as for those of you who don't. I'm writing this because I'm lucky enough to be able to, and because I want to. This band is an inspiration; they are the ideal. They've mastered their formula; they've achieved everything they set out to do and more. They've worked to be the best in the world at the one thing they put their minds to, and they've elevated their medium by driving this point into the ground. They've paid tribute to the legends that inspired them by being the direct living line from the past into the future. They've preserved their own myth by remaining mysterious—and they've done it all on their own terms. Their secret is simple yet too often overlooked by others who reach similar critical junctures: through the highs and lows, they've stuck to their guns and never, ever lost sight of who they are.

CHAPTER ONE

WHAT IT MEANS TO BE YOUNG

SOMETIMES IT REALLY IS all in the name—if the name is well chosen. Over the years, Angus and Malcolm Young have told two different stories of how AC/DC chose theirs, both of which involve a household appliance. According to one, they were hanging out in their sister Margaret's bedroom in Sydney, Australia, sometime in 1972, when they spotted the acronym for alternating current/direct current on the metal plate at the back of the family vacuum cleaner. The second version states that their sister-in-law spied it on the back of her sewing machine and suggested it to the boys when they realized that their new band couldn't be booked for gigs without a name. In both stories one truth remains the same: the Young brothers, who have always been the executive body in the band, chose to be represented by the universal symbol for the two types of electrical current that flow through the wires of common appliances and electrical equipment such as an electric guitar. One stream flows constantly in one direction, while the other alternately changes direction, but both of them carry an equal charge.

. . .

"AC/DC" was an easy choice for two young, hungry, erstwhile rock stars. It was a simple, graphically powerful logo, but it conveyed much more about them than they probably realized at the time. As randomly as their decision seemed to have been made, the two teenagers intuitively captured the essence of their band's sound as it would remain for the ensuing thirty-five years. Naming themselves after the electricity that powers their equipment was the perfect metaphor for everything AC/DC stands for, from their sheer power and bristling volume to their hard-wired dedication to blues and rock and roll. In choosing their name, they also set a precedent for how they would make band decisions: instinctually, definitively, and without overanalysis.

AC/DC has recorded fourteen studio albums full of songs that open, almost exclusively, with the searing crunch of one or both of the Young brothers' guitars. Considering that the band's entire catalog is built on four or five basic, frequently used rock and blues chords, it is impressive that they've managed to pen a catalog of riffs that never sound like anyone else while remaining less repetitive than logic would predict. Do the math: the brothers Young have written roughly 140 songs with a handful of basic power chords. Now take into account how many of those songs and chord progressions have become pillars of hard rock: "Highway to Hell," "Back in Black," "You Shook Me All Night Long," "T.N.T.," "Long Way to the Top," "Thunderstruck," "High Voltage," "If You Want Blood (You've Got It)," "Dirty Deeds," "For Those About to Rock (We Salute You)," "Hell's Bells," and many more. AC/DC's contribution to rock is gracefully zen: the Youngs and the band have made, and remade, iconic anthems from the most fundamental ingredients of the genre. They have not reinvented the wheel—they've spun it like a motherfucker.

The Young brothers' playing never strays far from the basics, but the pair employ riveting, incendiary anomalies that set them apart. For discussion's sake, let's start with "Shoot to Thrill" (the tablature of which can be found on page 666 of the *The Definitive AC/DC Songbook,* published by Amsco). The song opens with Malcolm Young's direct current: an A power chord rung out long and low. His brother soon joins in, splattering his alternating rhythm across the top of it as the band's rhythm section builds to a freight-train momentum, locked in perfect time. After two blistering verses and choruses, during which the two guitarists send up contrasting high- and low-tuned parts, the meat of the song falls out in the breakdown, revealing the beauty of the Youngs' interplay. Malcolm reiterates the gritty base chords, laying the foundation for his brother's solo—a rain-storm of clean, harmonic, plucked notes played on two strings at once. Led by Angus's rhythmic, finger-picked riff, the song ramps back into full swing and maximum volume. And on into the end.

The Youngs have built a legacy on lobbing riffs back and forth at each other with the ferocity of two seasoned tennis players competing in a title match. Their innate electricity is the alternating and direct current of the band: Malcolm drives ahead consistently, while his brother alternates wildly.

The hum of electric energy between them is palpable even in the studio recordings. "As far as guitar goes," says Guns N' Roses legend Slash, "it doesn't get any better. AC/DC is *the* guitar band. They were definitely a band I turned to when I was learning to play and finding my style. No one sounds like Malcolm and Angus. They've always done their thing and done it better than anyone else."

The two were born in Glasgow, Scotland, to William and Margaret Young—Malcolm in 1953 and Angus in 1955. They were the last of eight children. Their father, who had been a ground mechanic during World War II, found work hard to come by after the war, and opted to relocate the family to Sydney in 1963, where they could take advantage of the Australian government's immigration stimulus package. It was a new start for the Youngs, as Australia had been to UK citizens (and criminals) for two hundred years.

Unsurprisingly, music was a constant in the Young household. Malcolm and Angus's older brothers played accordion, saxophone, and guitar. Their sister, Margaret, the second oldest and the only girl in the family, influenced them with the jazz and blues records she favored, from Louis Armstrong and Robert Johnson to the early rock and roll of Fats Domino and Chuck Berry. Their brother Alex, however, was the first to turn his musical ability into a viable career: in the '60s he landed a job playing saxophone for Tony Sheridan, the English singer-songwriter best known for his collaboration with the Beatles back in their nascent Hamburg days. Alex was the only member of the family who remained in the UK when the Youngs emigrated, where he was subsequently signed to the Beatles label, Apple, as a singer-songwriter and member of the band Grapefruit.

Alex's accomplishments inspired George, the brother closest in age to Malcolm and Angus, to pursue his own musical dreams. George was an accomplished guitar player, and once the family was established in Sydney he threw himself into the city's music scene. He soon joined forces with four other children of postwar immigrants to found a band based on the British Invasion sound of the Beatles and the Rolling Stones. From the moment they came together in 1964 until they disbanded in 1969, the Easybeats were Australia's biggest pop band, and the first Aussie act to score an international pop hit with the song "Friday on My Mind," a classic of the era. The Easybeats were Australia's Beatles, and caused a similar degree of hysteria among teenage girls. Angus Young's earliest understanding of what it meant to be a rock star was formed after a teen magazine published his family's address, causing a mob of girls to set up camp outside, awaiting his brother's arrival. In an effort to elude them, he ducked around the block, jumped a neighbor's fence, and tried to sneak in the back door—to no avail. He'd been followed and was nearly run over by screaming girls who forced their way into the house in search of his brother. As surreal and titillating as the experience must have been, on a realistic level, George's success made a life in music seem attainable to his younger brothers. But that wasn't the only important lesson George handed down.

The Easybeats mined a sound that bands all over the

world were tapping into in the '60s, and they did it well, but nothing in their catalog touches the musicality of "Friday on My Mind." It is their most innovative track, and the only one relevant to a discussion of AC/DC. The song was written by George, who played rhythm guitar in the band, and his writing partner, Harry Vanda, who played lead. Much like Malcolm and Angus, the pair were the core of the Easybeats. There is a rhythmic plucking style to the guitar parts in "Friday on My Mind" that sets it apart from other British Invasion acts of the day such as the Animals, Donovan, and Herman's Hermits. Beneath the pretty harmonies, there is an urgency to the song, fueled by the frenetic dual-guitar romp that George Young's brothers later made the foundation of their sound. "Friday on My Mind" is structured like an AC/DC song as well, building from a simple alternating refrain into a two-part guitar swell capped by a shouted chorus. It is an ear-catching piece of music today as it was then. It's no wonder that when the Easybeats made their English debut at the Saville Theater in 1966, the Rolling Stones and the Beatles were seated in the first row. The band went on to tour with the Stones in '67, as "Friday on My Mind" was heard 'round the world. Unfortunately, the Easybeats couldn't build on their sudden success, and spent the next few years struggling to evolve before ultimately disbanding. After living abroad for a subsequent few years, George Young and Harry Vanda returned to Australia in 1973, ready to put together a new band. The pair discovered that George's two little brothers had been busy following in his footsteps—and had laid the groundwork for something else entirely.

In the years George had been away, Malcolm and Angus had taught themselves to play guitar quite proficiently. They'd never taken a lesson: they learned by listening to their siblings' records and every new one they could afford to buy. They learned as much from each other's unschooled techniques as they did from practicing alone, and developed a close musical relationship that became an unspoken language of which they were most likely unaware. Their symbiosis was based on necessity as well, since they shared the family's one acoustic guitar between them while learning the basics. Malcolm, who, growing up, was never much taller than his little brother (both are just five-feet-two today), learned to play open-string chords because his hands were too small to reach across the frets and properly hold down the thick strings of the acoustic in any kind of power chords. Malcolm's options changed around 1968, when George's bandmate, Harry Vanda, gave Malcolm a Gretsch Jet Firebird electric guitar. The thinner strings and shorter distance between the steel wire and the wood of the neck were easier to navigate, but by then his natural playing preferences were well established.

There was, however, more to learn. George taught Malcolm how to alter the sound of his electric guitar by changing the strings and tunings, and Malcolm used that knowledge to find a tone that suited him. He favored a no-frills grit antithetical to the glam rock of the time, opting to follow the lead of acts like Eric Clapton and John Mayall's Bluesbreakers, Peter Green, Paul Butterfield, and Mike Bloomfield. Malcolm gravitated toward the great bluesmen as well, from Muddy Waters and B.B. King to John Lee Hooker and Albert King. He was also moved by the sheer volume of the loudest of the English white-boy blues bands, integrating the best of the Who, the Stones, and Led Zeppelin into what became his signature style of rhythm guitar playing.

As loud as he ever was, Malcolm did not outshine the Young family's seventh son, wee Angus. Always smaller than his brothers, he was nonetheless tenacious as a pit bull—and once locked on target, just as focused. As a youth, he may have been the most diminutive in the family, but he was also the most feared. To paraphrase what his brothers have said, he never got into fights, because no one dared fight him. Still, Angus was far from a bad kid; he cared little then (and to this day) for drinking, drugs, or excess. He was the most artistically inclined of his brothers, spending his spare time sketching and painting, as he does to this day. As a young man he was consumed with tea, milk shakes, cigarettes, chocolate, and playing his guitar every waking moment. He cites Chuck Berry and Little Richard as his earliest influences, and says that once his older brother Alex taught him a simple twelve-bar blues riff, he was off and running. It was virtually the only lesson he ever got. By the time he was fifteen, Angus's scholastic record was so poor that he anticipated his inevitable dismissal by seeking menial jobs in butcher shops, local factories, and eventually a neighborhood printer's shop. His focus remained unchanged, however, and as his playing progressed, he began to learn lead-guitar riffs by plucking along on the family banjo—a trait that has remained a centerpiece of his style. You can hear it in his hornet's-nest introduction to "Thunderstruck" and the jumpy harmonic riffing of "Who Made Who"—everywhere in his repertoire, Angus's banjo roots are there.

As teens, the two youngest Youngs found their way into bands that, in name at least, were as iconoclastic as they themselves were to become. Malcolm's most notable outfit was called the Velvet Underground, and was completely unlike the iconic New York City band of the same name. Angus's first serious band was called Kantuckee, named after the most popular fried chicken chain in Australia. The brothers never saw themselves playing in a band together, although they spent the time away from their bands playing together and analyzing the artists of the day they deemed worthy, from Mountain to Cactus, Argent, and Deep Purple, as well as Hendrix, the Stones, and Jeff Beck.

The return of their brother George changed everything, as he saw something they didn't: Malcolm and Angus were polished enough to be recorded professionally. George and his writing partner in the Easybeats, Harry Vanda, had returned to finish an album they'd been working on in London, and rather than troll for local musicians that suited them, they enlisted Malcolm and Angus. The resulting album, *The Tales of Old Grand-Daddy*, was recorded over a month's time in EMI Studios in Australia, when the pair were just twenty and eighteen. The experience made playing music professionally, as a proper job, one step more real to them. Afterward they returned to their own bands, but the seeds were sown. At their brother George's urging, Angus and Malcolm finally got together to form what would become AC/DC.

George was the band's guide and mentor: he found his brothers other local players to round out their lineup, he helped them to book gigs, and he acted as manager. He filled in on bass when needed, he gave them writing advice, and he went on to produce, often with Harry Vanda, the majority of the band's albums. It was also George who suggested that Malcolm and Angus follow a few iron-cast ground rules when writing music: to keep them from killing each other, as young, hotheaded brothers are likely to do, he suggested that Malcolm occupy an area of the house that his younger, more frenetic brother was forbidden to enter. With George's guidance, by November 1973 the initial AC/DC lineup, featuring vocalist Dave Evans, bassist Larry Van Krent, and drummer Colin Burgess, was locked down. They played their first show on New Year's Eve of that year. As is often the case, it took a few permutations to get everything right. It would be a few years before the Youngs found their muse in singer Bon Scott, and a few more before drummer Phil Rudd joined the ranks. It took a few more after that to land bassist Cliff Williams, which made their historic lineup whole. But that night, as 1973 turned to 1974, that didn't matter—that night history began.

No one sounds like Malcolm and Angus. I remember Mötley Crüe was recording *Dr. Feelgood* in Little Mountain

Studios in Vancouver when they were recording *The Razor's Edge*, in about 1988. I was such a fan, I had to ask Malcolm if I could buy one of his guitars—I just had to. It was an old, beat-up Gretsch and he'd taken all the front pickups out so that it sounded all fucking gnarly and crunchy as shit. Malcolm has the best voice, it's like Keith Richards's. There's just no one else in the world that sounds like that. I asked him if I could buy it and he was like, "Ay-kay, mate, you can 'ave dis one." I plugged that thing in and it didn't matter what chord I played—it immediately sounded like AC/DC. That guitar had no fucking choice! But you know what? I can't fucking find that thing *anywhere*. Somebody boosted it off me somewhere along the line. Fuck! Hey, whoever you are— thanks a lot, *asshole*!

—Tommy Lee, drummer, Mötley Crüe

A cornerstone of the Young brothers' legacy is the direct simplicity of their playing. They followed a hand-picked tradition of their own, tracing a line from Chuck Berry through the distorted blues of Hendrix and '60s chord smashers like the Who. They also took after electric blues greats like Albert and Freddie King, who valued clarity and volume and a less-is-more approach to bending notes to convey a song's emotional story. As far back as 1973, AC/DC established themselves as a no-frills, musically adept, tough-as-nails rock band. They have always been very straightforward, though more often than not they've been misunderstood.

As AC/DC became known outside of Australia, they

were thought to be aligned with the English punk movement. Aside from working-class roots and a take-no-prisoners attitude that mirrored those of the punks, AC/DC's self-taught musicianship was leagues beyond the amateur do-it-yourself level of playing in the early punk scene. In punk it wasn't what you played (if you even could play)—it was *how* you did it. By contrast, in AC/DC they played as skillfully as they performed. They were definitely an inspiration to punk rock, but they were as alien to the scene as Queen Elizabeth.

In the same vein, throughout the '70s and '80s and into today, AC/DC has been regarded as one of the forefathers of heavy metal. Considering the clear blues tradition in the music, it's an odd characterization. Metal guitar playing is defined by tapping, sweep-picking, and rapid-fire displays of virtuosity that stylistically have nothing to do with traditional rock or AC/DC. And as much as the band's singers screamed and wailed, their inclination toward harmony is antithetical to heavy metal's songbook. The only trait that AC/DC and metal as we know it today have in common is that both celebrate the power of interlocking guitar parts. If anything, that is AC/DC's legacy for metal: unlike anyone before them, they married the looser bluesy dynamics of Led Zeppelin with the dark, individualistic riffing of Black Sabbath.

"AC/DC in general as a band falls through the cracks for some reason, and Angus as a guitarist just doesn't get the notoriety he deserves," says Robin Stone, associate professor of guitar at Boston's renowned Berklee College of Music. "Their music is straightforward, but that shouldn't have anything to do with it. It's a strange thing among guitar players that they don't recognize Angus as a really cool player for just that fact. Obviously they're a popular band with the public, but guitar players seem to think that simplicity has no value. I've argued to the point of pulling my hair out with some of my students about why B.B. King has value. It seems that a lot of players only see the value in the melodic shredder stuff of the eighties or the really dark stuff that is what metal is all about today. There is so much more to the guitar than that."

Though AC/DC's songs tend to rely on five or six guitar chords at most, those chords are the very pillars of rock and roll: E, A, D, G, C, and B. But what the Youngs have found a way to do for the past thirty-five years is to come up with subtle, well-placed anomalies that make the simple sublime. These chord-based songs are instantly recognizable for their unity and power, with each band member lending a clearly discernible part to a syncopated whole. Each song is structured so that it carefully builds to a climax—and repeats. "A chord riff as opposed to a note riff is instantly recognizable," Professor Stone says. "Think of the opening of Led Zeppelin's 'Heartbreaker,' that's Jimmy Page playing a note riff. Now think of 'Back in Black' or 'Highway to Hell.' Those are really cool chords that start off an interplay between Malcolm and Angus. They both work at the opening to engage the listener, but they do so in a very different way. When you hear a note-based guitar riff, I think the listener's tendency is to react to it more objectively. The feeling is, 'Wow, that's cool playing,' because it engages your mind in one way. When you hear chords like AC/DC's, cranked to maximum volume, it is something else entirely. You are literally, almost physically, grabbed by it."

AC/DC emerged at a time when hard rock was going through a transition. Bands such as Led Zeppelin and the Who had planted the seeds by creating a modern, edgy, overdriven take on rock, rhythm, and blues. But by the '70s, both groups had veered off into very different territory. Zeppelin's exploration of drugs and dark magic led them up the stairway to heaven and over misty mountains, where they absorbed influences as wide-ranging as American country, Middle Earth, and Moroccan hash to flavor their stylish, English take on the blues. The Who, for their part, went down the rock opera rabbit hole in the late '60s only to emerge as a more progressively inclined, uneven version of themselves. Meanwhile, Black Sabbath had whipped their minimal, nihilist blues into a cocaine-fueled paranoia. There was no other band at the time carrying the torch of tradition.

"You have to draw a parallel line connecting the Who and AC/DC because they have a very similar chordal vamp style," says Professor Stone. "But in terms of rock history, AC/DC represent something else. They fit in between Led Zeppelin and Van Halen. Eddie Van Halen became the big monster guitar player of his generation, but they had this whole other pop appeal. AC/DC was much closer to the foundations of hard rock, like the Who. Think of tunes like 'Baba O'Reilly' or 'Won't Get Fooled Again,' then think of 'For Those About to Rock.' We are talking about the same kind of anthem."

That unmistakable chordal element in AC/DC's music is positively Malcolm Young. Unlike other rhythm guitar players, his contributions are truly the soul of the band, rooting the songs as fundamentally as only a bass player usually can. Malcolm Young has cowritten every huge hit in the canon, and plays most of the riffs that the fans know and love. He couldn't be more essential to AC/DC, or more of an icon of rhythm guitar playing in the rock-and-roll genre. Malcolm's round, deep, rhythmic tone is as unique as his brother Angus's hyperactive solos, but it's not due to his guitar pickups alone. There is something extraordinary in Malcolm's choices as a guitar player. There are many ways to play chords, but only Malcolm's fingering decisions and strumming technique create the dynamic resonance in AC/DC. "A good rhythm guitarist shakes the neck a bit so chords vibrate the right way, because you can't just play a chord straight and expect it to have any style," Professor Stone says. "There's also the right-hand element that Malcolm has. He hits the strings and mutes them a certain way and does some extra attacks, as we call them, when he hits certain chords. That is how he fills in the rhythmic space. There is also the way he wiggles his left hand on the guitar neck to make the notes sing out a bit—that's all his own. He brings his playing to life in that way."

His brother's signature sound is equally unique. While

Malcolm commands a rich, gritty depth, his brother Angus is a master of clear, piercing frenzy. Angus has more or less always played a Gibson SG, a guitar that features two Humbucker pickups located side by side under the main surface area of the strings. For the record, Humbuckers are hyper-responsive, much more so than the single-coil pickups featured in Stratocasters, the guitar favored by Eric Clapton and Jimi Hendrix. They've been the pickup of choice for every hard rock and metal band in modern times, from Guns N' Roses to Aerosmith, because they provide, without fail, and with no effects, that old-fashioned, thick rock sound. The Gibson SG's double coil delivers twofold, lending the player an incredibly wired, loud, fat, and clean tone as a result of the increased magnetic field. In Angus's case, however, his equipment is just one piece of the puzzle; his SG is merely a megaphone.

A guitar player's vibrato is, in essence, their voice. It is how they speak through their instrument. Every player's vibrato is distinct and unique because only their fingers and touch can create it. If Chuck Berry, Eddie Van Halen, Jimmy Page, Eric Clapton, and Angus Young all played the same guitar lick note for note, you can be sure that none of them would sound the same.

"Everybody's got their own distinctive way of using vibrato," Professor Stone says. "Vibrato is, in simplest terms, how you touch the strings and create the sound you create. Players can have a slow one or a rapid one. Just think of someone like B.B. King. He's got a whole range of them that are distinctly his own. Angus Young has a rapid vibrato, which shouldn't surprise anyone, because he's so hyper. Just watch him playing live! He's a nut—he does the duckwalk back and forth and over the course of a concert he's just out there. I don't even know how he plays that well, moving around so much. But think about it: all of that energy is coming through him into his hand, so he's got a singing, fairly rapid vibrato style that is very unique to him. Other people can do that stuff, and play his licks, but they'll never get Angus's tone. To me, Angus is the guitar player that sits between Page and Van Halen. But I have to say, Angus is a much cleaner player than Jimmy Page, hands down. Technically, Jimmy is actually pretty sloppy. Angus is much more refined; his phrasing always fits right into the rhythm, and he's always in time."

Malcolm and Angus Young have managed to do more with three chords than any other human beings have ever done. I admire them for their creativity with the use of the A, C, D, and the occasional E chord. That's all they needed because they're so fucking good at delivering their style. Nobody can touch them and nobody should try. Their music might sound repetitive in some instances, but when you put AC/DC on, you can't deny what you hear. It's just 'This is what you get.' You get that sound, you get that delivery that has been perfected. And what they give you always delivers. I think they're fucking great.

—Slash

Angus and Malcolm's interplay can be easily understood, even by those who know nothing about playing guitar because of the sonically honest manner in which they've always been recorded. Whether you take AC/DC in live or on record, the brothers' roles are best deconstructed via a simple rule of thumb. The studio recordings, for the most part, feature the band as they are onstage, from their point of view: you will hear Malcolm's guitar parts in the right speaker and Angus's on the left. It makes consuming AC/DC all the more a spectator sport.

In concert, from the audience's perspective, Malcolm is on the left, situated along the back line with bass player Cliff Williams. It's where he belongs—his playing is as fundamentally essential to the band's rhythm as the drums and bass. His counterpoint, Angus, is on the right—chronically. Over the course of a typical 90- to 120-minute-plus AC/DC show, the guitarist races around the stage, moons the audience, runs up and around the drum riser, and spins on the ground like a frenzied imp—all without missing a note. He's now fifty-four and has yet to change his act.

As loud and chaotic as AC/DC ever becomes, live or on record, the two guitarists never fall out of time with each other. They never rely on dissonance to prove a point, only finely tuned distortion. Much like Phil Spector's Wall of Sound, where the producer layered and intertwined vocal harmonies and orchestral instrumentation to create a sonic tapestry, Malcolm's and Angus's parts always merge to become a greater rhythmic whole as the song evolves. The two are perfectly matched and versatile in their style, able to drop in and out of each other's playing so organically that once a song has begun, the rhythm driving it seems to be handed off between them as easily as two average Joes shake hands or high-five.

The first time Mötley Crüe met AC/DC we were on the bill with them and Van Halen for the Monsters of Rock in 1984. Nikki Sixx and I were in our drunken, biting-people, rage tour. We would just go up and bite every idol we had and every person that we met that we decided we loved. So, backstage at that show, Nikki bit Eddie Van Halen and he started freaking out. So Nikki turned away from him and started walking toward Malcolm. Now, Nikki is a big dude—he's six feet tall and he's always been kind of large. And Malcolm and Angus are maybe six feet tall put together. Malcolm sees him coming and he's not fucking having it. You know what they say, man, it's not the size of the dog in the fight, it's the size of the fight in the dog. Malcolm just looks at him and goes, "You fucking bite me, mate, and I will fucking *kill* you." Nikki just stopped in his tracks. That was the end of that shit.

—Tommy Lee

Angus Young occupies a unique role in rock history: he is the only guitarist whose onstage persona has outshone that of his band's lead singer. (Two of them, actually.) From the start, Angus has epitomized the manic, electric rock-and-roll possession that is AC/DC. His schoolboy uniform is as well known as the band's logo, but it wasn't as natural a fit as the band's name; it took a few incarnations for Angus to find his performance character. The fact that, from the start, he wanted to become something other than himself onstage speaks volumes, however. His instrument isn't what does him in: while recording, writing, or practicing, he prefers to sit still. It is the thrill of performance, of broadcasting the music to the masses, that compels him to become a man possessed. Even now, at fifty-four, he is a testament to the raw, transformative power of rock and roll.

There is no other way to start a conversation about AC/DC than with a discussion of the Young brothers' guitar playing. The way they hit the strings *is* AC/DC. They are the electricity, they are the inspiration, they are the devotion to the cause. They absorbed the kind of playing that mattered to them—the clean, amplified, individualistic playing of the blues—that they fused with the boogie-woogie of Chuck Berry and '70s rock to create a sound that no one has ever done better.

"Malcolm and Angus go together like hand in glove," says Professor Stone. "Just like the Van Halen brothers, they produce stuff that works *so* well. They are two guitarists who play two distinctive parts, and in most of their songs find a way to combine them. They are very much intertwined and interlocked, working together really well and sounding great doing it. Personally, I believe that there is a genetic link among siblings that cannot be duplicated. Siblings who learn to play music together achieve some bizarre rhythmic combinations that work well for them but almost don't make sense on paper. If you try to play their parts in a band, you will often be puzzled, wondering just how they do it. And no matter how skilled you are technically, you won't figure it out. Players who aren't related can have that kind of luck, too—and any that do should stay together! But my experience has shown me that siblings seem to have that kind of bond organically if they've grown up learning to play together. They have access to something that is a human language unto itself."

CHAPTER TWO

GONNA BE A ROCK 'N' ROLL SINGER

A ROCK-AND-ROLL BAND

is like a gang, a clan, or a family—often a dysfunctional one—that comes together to say something. Whether their message is revolutionary or nothing new at all matters just as much as—or as little as—or even less than—*how* they say it. In popular music, the message isn't simply in the words and music; the musicians are the message, too. They are representatives of the point of view, the opinions expressed, and the stories told in the music they create. Whether their image is manufactured, imposed, or an organic extension of the artist's or band's personality, it is their most powerful tool. As loud as their sound might be, their image will always be louder. Even nonimagery, like the nihilist minimalism of Nine Inch Nails' bare, square fonts on black backgrounds, is akin to iconography. That lack of adornment and the mechanical acronym NIN screams the band's identity as well as a detailed manifesto would. To that end, to the public at large, the lead singer of a band has been and always will be more than just the one who delivers the vocals. Whether they like it or not, the lead singer is *the* face in the crowd: they are out in front representing the band in every way. Whether they write the songs, the lyrics, or none of it, the lead singer is a band's mascot, their living bullhorn, and their in-house press agent.

AC/DC, however, never needed a mascot: from the start, Angus Young's onstage persona fit the bill, setting the bar high for any singer hoping to share the stage with him. Showing him up would be impossible, so the singer needed to fulfill that role another way. The Young brothers' guitar synergy demanded a singer with volume, style, attitude, and presence enough to carve a niche through the caterwaul. The band's first singer, Dave Evans, was capable enough vocally, but his glam rock stylings were lost in AC/DC's sound. His voice was bluesy but too delicate to keep up. Evans had to push himself just to be heard over the music and frequently suffered laryngitis on tour—a condition the Youngs particularly had no sympathy for. They expected their singer to convey a take-no-prisoners image as rough and resilient as their playing. Laryngitis didn't fit into that equation. Until they could find a proper replacement, AC/DC would never be quite what it could be.

It took two singers with incredible physical ability and undeniable integrity to helm AC/DC, each in their own distinct, dissimilar way. By all accounts, Bon Scott was very different from Brian Johnson, but each was the only man capable of existing in a band with two brothers as tenacious and opinionated as the Youngs. They are also the only two singers I've ever heard with perfectly eroded yet robust vocal chords: Bon in his time and Brian still today is capable of a vocal style that is as difficult to attain as it is to maintain. "It's hard for me to even analyze what is going on vocally in AC/DC," says Diane Stewart, associate professor of voice at the Berklee College of Music, "mostly because I find myself just sitting there and enjoying it. The first thing I tell my students who want to sing in that blues rock tradition is that by doing so, they are going to limit the colors in their voice, by which I mean the sounds they can make. Singing that way will limit the styles of music they will be able to do in their lifetime. It will lock them into that sound because after a while it is all that their voice will physically be able to do. You also have to realize that people's physiologies are different and that some people can take the kind of abuse that comes with hard rock singing for longer than others, because their bodies are different. If some people do it for even a short period of time they may lose a significant portion of their singing range. I tell my students about what the consequences are, but the truth is, it's hard for me to tell anyone not to sing like that if they want to, because I like the way it sounds, even though it certainly isn't good for your voice."

A singer's tonal quality is a completely idiosyncratic phenomenon determined by the vibration of the vocal folds, two mucous membranes stretched across the larynx in the human throat. The vocal folds modulate the flow of air from the lungs: upon inhalation they open, they close when a breath is held, and on exhalation they vibrate and create a sound. The speed of the air rushing through the space between them is one of many factors that determine the pitch of a singing voice. The size of the throat, the nose, and the lungs of the singer also plays a part in the resulting sound. In addition to the vocal folds, which are known as the "true vocal chords," there is also a set of vestibular folds, which are mucous membranes situated above the true vocal chords to protect them. The vestibular folds are used when screaming, and when damaged they can regenerate, unlike the "true" vocal chords. If pushed to their limits, however, the vestibular folds can suffer permanent damage, causing the true vocal chords to suffer as well.

Neither the late Bon Scott nor his replacement, Brian Johnson, took vocal lessons, but both of them discovered, most likely by singing through ratty sound systems in dive bars, the secret to sustaining a career as a rock singer: breath control. Using the diaphragm, the layer of muscle between the lungs and the stomach, to regulate the passage of air is essential to a singer's power—and career longevity. In order to hit a range of notes and to sustain a vocal line over the course of a song, vocalists must ration their air, planning accordingly so that they hit their hardest notes with an ample supply of it. Doing so properly takes the strain off the true vocal chords by ensuring that the air is pushed through at a slow, even rate rather than forced through in a rush or, even worse, pushed out in an underpowered gasp. Sustaining notes improperly puts the burden on the vocal chords by causing a rapid vibration that leads directly to permanent damage. Learning to store air in the deepest part of the lungs, at the lowest points where they expand into the back, behind the stomach and up against the diaphragm, is the key to a powerful vocal performance over the course of a song and a career. Any singers who solely utilize the upper chest to harbor their breath are crippling themselves. They will never sing with all their power and are sure to suffer vocal nodes—the earliest sign of permanent damage—much sooner. Nodes are literally a singer's worst enemy. They develop on overworked vocal chords much the way calluses develop on overworked hands, disturbing the natural vibration of the chords and limiting the range, depth, and unique tonal characteristics of the voice. Everything else passing through the singer's throat can play a part in damaging their instrument as well, from alcohol and drugs to cigarette smoke, as can speaking often (and loudly) between singing performances. To say the least, being a professional rock singer comes with every occupational hazard to their instrument known to man. Considering that Bon Scott was a drinker and that Brian enjoys both cigarettes and alcohol, the fact that both men could deliver such powerful performances live and on record over time is astounding. Neither took a lesson, but they clearly learned, instinctually, how to wring the most from their abilities without losing them.

"When I listen to Brian Johnson, I'm struck by how amazing and unusual it is that he can have that much power, because I understand that he smokes quite a bit," Professor Stewart says. "He has achieved a degree of permanent damage to his voice while maintaining his ability to hit notes. There is only one way that I can think to explain that—there is something that is extraordinary about him and his breath control. He is not a young man, and any singer who has been able to have a long career singing that way has either been trained to do so, which I don't think he has, or they just naturally know a lot about managing air. What is most amazing about Brian, though, is his intonation. As someone who sang rock for many years myself, I know from experience that usually by the third or fourth night laryngitis becomes a real issue. When I listen to Brian I can't help but think, 'How is he hitting the intonation so spot on? How does he do that night after night?' "

If a professor of voice doesn't know the answer, I certainly don't. Brian himself has never revealed any Jedi secret knowledge, either. Some things must just be understood and appreciated for what they are, and both the late Ronald Belford "Bon" Scott and Brian Johnson are vocalists in a class by themselves. Their singing voices are as raw and gritty as an old bar floor, as menacing as a thief in an alley, and as crisp as a crack of lightning. They took to their jobs differently, but they are the only two men that could have fronted a powerhouse band like AC/DC and hammered the point home. They never just kept up; they broadcast the message loud and clear.

> Bon Scott was fucking awesome. He was to hard rock and heavy metal what Jim Morrison was to rock and roll and poetry. He was just amazing.
>
> —Slash

Born in Scotland in 1946, Ronald Belford Scott's family relocated to Australia when he was six, first landing in Melbourne before relocating to Perth, over two thousand miles away, ten years later. Scott was an outcast in his new home. Thanks to his Scottish accent, he stood out in school, and, to differentiate him from a classmate named Ron, he was nicknamed Ronnie "Bonnie," which is slang for his homeland. Always the proud Scotsman, at age twelve Bon joined his father in the Fremantle Scots Pipe Band, where he played drums from 1958 through 1963. As his AC/DC bandmates later discovered—much to their bewilderment—during the recording of "It's a Long Way to the Top," on their debut album, *High Voltage,* Bon never learned to play a note on the bagpipe during his five-year tenure in the Scots Pipe Band. He hadn't even tried. He did his homeland proud, however, by learning to play the solo for the song, both on record and in concert. Onstage it was an impressive exertion for someone holding down the vocals, one that nearly caused him to pass out on several occasions. He always did his best to deliver, despite the fact that timing the bagpipe exhalations couldn't be less suited to the tempo of rock and roll. As he told the press at the time, playing the bagpipe onstage was as problematic as "making love to an octopus."

Bon was a born rocker who got a tattoo and an earring as soon as he could. At age eighteen, in 1964, he made his first public appearance as a singer with his band the Spektors (named after legendary producer Phil Spector), at a venue called Port Beach Stomp in Perth. The band didn't go far; apparently the greatest obstacle to their musical evolution was the fact that Bon was in reform school at the time and could only play or rehearse on the weekends. He'd landed himself there for stealing a car with a few friends and driving it off the Fremantle Bridge into the harbor. Once the Spektors disbanded in 1966, Bon went on to sing and drum in the Valentines, a band who devoted themselves to covering soul artists such as Wilson Pickett and Sam and Dave. They were signed to a record deal soon after, and landed an opening gig for the Easybeats in 1967, an evening during which Bon befriended guitarist George Young. George, who already had a desire to produce and nurture up-and-coming talent, took the Valentines under his wing; with his help they recorded a George Young original called "She Said," which featured Bon playing recorder and singing. George Young knew what he was doing, because "She Said" and another song, "Every Day I Have to Cry," became instant radio hits in western Australia, so to build on their success, the Valentines relocated to Melbourne, which has always been a critical music center at the national level. At that point, Bon gave up drumming and began singing full-time in the band.

Though they focused their sound toward a more distinctly rock-and-roll feel, the Valentines found little success in their new hometown, so they shifted gears and temporarily relocated again, this time to Sydney. The music scene was more mainstream there, which allowed them to return to playing mostly cover tunes while dressing in shiny outfits, in keeping with the bubblegum pop style of the day. Though he was forced to toe a squeaky-clean line onstage to pay the bills, Bon was a different man entirely in his off hours. He became a local legend known for his devotion to excess in all things, his skill in a street fight, and his loyalty to his friends above all. Perhaps that loyalty explains his dedication to the Valentines, a group with whom he did not see eye to eye musically in any way, shape, or form. With one exception, his bandmates showed no desire to venture outside of the teen pop realm where they'd found financial success, despite Bon's efforts to turn the band toward more sexually charged, bluesier material. It's unknown exactly who was to blame for the sullying of the Valentines' image, but after becoming the first Australian band to be arrested for possession of marijuana, they broke up in 1970, after which time Bon joined the Fraternity, a group with whom he enjoyed further national success. The Fraternity was a more serious, bucolic, progressive rock outfit along the lines of the Band. They developed a sizable local fan base and toured briefly with Jerry Lee Lewis as his support act, but they failed to find the success that other, less worthy acts were enjoying around them.

Hoping to expand their horizons, the Fraternity relocated to the UK for a time, just after Bon married his girlfriend, Irene. The entire Fraternity, as it were, lived in London, in a suburban, unheated, three-story house filled with seventeen of their crew and loved ones. They rehearsed regularly, took opening gigs for any well-known local band that would have them, and managed, after a period of relative inactivity, to book a brief German tour. In a desperate attempt to get more local work, they changed their name to Fang in 1973, hoping to align themselves with popular hard rock bands of the day such as Slade and Status Quo. It really didn't help much, and as things got worse, Bon began to support himself and his bandmates by tending bar in the neighborhood pub. One gig Fang did land, however, was fateful: opening up as the support band for an act named Geordie at Torquay Town Hall. That night, Bon was blown away by the group's jovial, raspy-voiced vocalist—a fellow named Brian Johnson. The two became fast friends over the course of that night and the next night as once again their bands shared a bill. Though they spent just two days fraternizing and performing, Bon never forgot Brian.

The Fraternity left the UK soon after and, upon returning home to Australia, broke and no further along than when they'd left, relocated again—this time to Adelaide, in hopes of once more starting anew. Bon must have known that something wasn't right, because he began to take every opportunity to record and write with friends in other bands. He dove into the music scene headfirst and became a huge fan of a group called the Coloured Balls, whose members wore vaguely droogish *Clockwork Orange* stage attire and played ear-melting rock at maximum volume. Bon showed up at every gig, often jammed with them onstage, and told every close associate that he'd quit the Fraternity tomorrow to be in a band like that. He clearly yearned to be more menacingly theatrical onstage.

Another event inspired Bon to take his life a bit more—if that was possible—by the balls. Not long after his return home, Bon nearly killed himself while driving his motorcycle drunk after a fight with his wife. He fell off the bike after sideswiping a car and losing control; he lost numerous teeth, broke his collarbone, scarred his neck, and wound up in a coma for three days, during which time he flatlined several times. As anyone would be, he was a changed man afterward, from his limp and cane to the loss of his bravado. Bon was unable to return to his job as a commercial fisherman, which had long been his favored nonmusical occupation. Instead he made money putting up posters advertising upcoming shows for Vince Lovegrove, his closest friend in the Valentines, who had since become a manager and booking agent for rock bands. Lovegrove had been a friend to Bon for years, loaning him money and giving him a place to sleep when he needed one, and during this time, Lovegrove was there once again. The unflappable Bon was definitely down, but being around the music kept his spirits up. One of the posters he hung was going to change his life, though he didn't pay it any mind at the time. It was just another cardboard ad he tacked to a telephone pole, this one advertising an upcoming show by a Sydney band of teenagers called AC/DC.

Lovegrove knew the Youngs and knew that they were unhappy with their founding singer, Dave Evans. He also knew that Bon *needed* a band, so he played middleman, telling each party about the other. Their initial reactions were not promising. Bon thought that the Youngs were just that—too young to be in a band with him; and the Youngs believed that Bon was too old. Lovegrove trusted his instincts, however, and assigned Bon to be their guide and driver during their stay in Adelaide. Legend has it that when they first met, all that Bon would talk about was how irritated he was because he'd put his wife's underwear on by mistake that morning. Apparently it was a hot day, and under his jeans his lady's briefs were chafing him to high heaven. It was just the type of charm that won Scott as many friends as it did land him in fights in his life. In spite of his doubts about the Youngs, Bon went on to treat the job as an audition, providing the band with drinks and joints at too-early hours of the morning and dropping endless hints about his skills as a drummer and singer. He took in AC/DC's show from the front of the stage, laughing maniacally at Angus's nonstop overdrive, and was further impressed by him when Angus challenged a group of hecklers, all of whom were much bigger than he, to have a go at him. He was the smallest and most fearless guy in the place.

After the show, an inebriated Bon told the Young brothers that if they wanted to really learn how to rock and roll, he was willing to give them a lesson—right away. They headed to the basement studio of one of his Fraternity bandmates' homes and jammed until the sun came up. Bon started out on drums until, after two songs, he was none-too-politely informed that AC/DC had a drummer and what they really needed was a singer. Scott didn't need much encouragement. He took to the microphone and gave a performance so intense that AC/DC's manager, Dennis Laughlin, offered him the job on the spot. He didn't take it, but said he'd consider it while the band was away. The next day they departed for a six-week residency in Perth, forty-two hours by road across some of the most barren and dangerous desert in Australia. The tour conditions and the relentless gig schedule ignited the already strained relationship between the Youngs and Dave Evans into one of open hostility. When they finally returned to Adelaide, on their way back to Sydney, they played a few shows, during all of which Bon got up and sang several songs with the band. He hadn't yet committed to the job, but if Evans hadn't suspected it already, they couldn't have sent him a bigger hint that he was done.

AC/DC did for Bon Scott what it has done for its fans for three decades: it hardwired him back into the excitement he first felt from music. He had a talent for rhythm and for singing and devoted himself to it completely, as he had already devoted himself to a life of adventure. That came easy; music did not, but after many false starts, Bon had finally found his place. Working with much younger rock and rollers (he was twenty-eight, while Malcolm was twenty and Angus was just eighteen) full of adolescent vinegar allowed him to write off-color, funny songs like "She's Got Balls"—something he'd never have been able to do with his more serious peers in the Fraternity. "She's Got Balls" was his first collaboration with the Youngs, after which their new singer began to pen lyrics rapidly, on the fly, often on the way to gigs. The synergy for both sides was finally just right and, as it does when the ingredients are present and in proper proportion, it all came together quickly.

Bon completed the AC/DC picture both in substance and image. He was the outlaw rock-and-roll front man—and leader—that they desperately needed. He guzzled cases of bourbon, he took methedrine, and he smoked dope. He lived the life *and* knew how to front the circus. He was something between an older brother and an elder statesman for the Youngs and he took to it with gusto. Joining the band spelled the end of his marriage to Irene, which was most likely for the best, considering how much of a sex symbol he soon became and how much he enjoyed the spoils of war, so to speak. Both Youngs have told tales of Bon being solicited not only by women, but also frequently by husbands asking him to do them the pleasure of pleasuring their wives. Scott adored young girls as much as they adored him, had little regard for girls' boyfriends, and on many an occasion on the road was quite literally run out of town. When he and the Youngs lived together in several houses in Melbourne, Bon was the ringleader who brought the party with him wherever he went, approaching every new situation as an experience to be indulged in to the fullest, immediately.

Bon's natural wit, charisma, and experience took AC/DC to another level, more or less right away, which is something that might have taken them years—and most likely several more singers—to otherwise achieve. Bon was the consummate '70s hard rock front man. He brought a sense of vaudevillian showmanship, a poet's eye for storytelling, and an unequaled vocal range to the music. He also added humor, a sly, untrustworthy charm, and a sense of danger to the proceedings, none of which was calculated. It was simply who he was.

"I rate Bon Scott as one of the greatest rock singers of all time," says Professor Stewart of the Berklee College of Music. "He had a wide, varied sound and was capable of a diverse palate of colors as a rock vocalist. He was also tremendously funny as a lyricist. I've always enjoyed AC/DC for having a sense of humor, for making fun of themselves and everything else. Bon was particularly good at that lyrically. Far too many rock bands today take themselves too seriously. I don't know what I'm going to do if I see another shot of a new band looking completely unamused. The thing I miss the most in rock and roll is an abundance of people who can laugh at themselves. Bon Scott and AC/DC could always definitely do that."

Bon scribbled the lines that became his lyrics, which he called "toilet poetry," in notebooks he carried with him almost everywhere. He'd begun recording episodes from his life in disjointed verse that way in his teens, and his natural zeal for adventures in the extreme made his jottings ready-to-record rock anthems. "She's Got Balls," for example, was written for his ex-wife. With lines like "She's got style my woman, makes me smile that woman," it's hardly a kiss-off to an ex. It's an ode to what was great about her, the subtext being that despite her great qualities, nothing could have kept him from leaving her. "She's Got Balls" was a tossed-off effort, however, and is hardly Bon Scott in his prime as a lyricist. At his best, Bon's evocative, visual stories were just the starting block for his nimble, powerful voice. He was incredibly adept at highlighting the finer points of the lyrical journey through the phrases he chose to emphasize. They weren't typical, but they were innately well placed, and as catchy and immediate as Angus's hooks and leads. But beyond that, Scott's raw sleaze and honesty were a tractor beam. It's simple: with Bon Scott, what you hear is what you get. He did not create imaginary heroes; he is the subject and narrator of his songs, telling the listener, without compromise, just how things are.

We can gain a deeper understanding of Bon's style as a

songwriter and a front man by tracing the influence in him of two of his musical idols: Jerry Lee Lewis and Alex Harvey. Jerry Lee Lewis's wild-eyed rock and roll epitomized the bad boy as bard. Known as "The Killer," Jerry Lee was immediately a musician as notorious as his songs were incendiary, one known as much for his engagement to his underage first cousin Myra Gale Brown as he was for setting his piano aflame onstage when given second billing to Chuck Berry. Lewis's lust for life conflicted with his strict Christian upbringing (his cousin is televangelist Jimmy Swaggart), lending his overtly sexual boogie-woogie rock and roll, from "Whole Lotta Shakin' " to "High School Confidential," an unmistakable heat. Similarly, when Bon Scott sang about a woman with "The Jack," he was shooting from the hip. In the song he relates a tale of losing a game of cards to a poker-faced woman, but the double entendre of lines like "Poker straight was her game, if she knew she could get you" becomes even more edgy if you are aware that "the jack" is Australian slang for the clap, or gonorrhea. (Scott was no stranger to the disease; in fact, the local clinic near the band's first house in Melbourne knew him by name, rather than by the anonymous numbers other patients were given upon arrival.) Bon did not simply regard Jerry Lee Lewis as a songwriting idol from a distance. He discovered that "The Killer" lived as he wrote when the Fraternity supported him on a tour of Australia. The two quickly became inseparable drinking buddies, so much so that after a few weeks, both bands' tour managers worked together to keep them clear of each other—and a supply of bourbon—to no avail.

If Jerry Lee was Bon Scott's spiritual guide in life and lyrics, an equally important influence was Alex Harvey. Harvey, a fellow Scot, began his musical career as a trumpet player with roots in Dixieland jazz and skiffle, which is a fusion of folk, blues, jazz, and country that originated in the United States in the '20s and became very popular in the UK in the '50s. A close kin to jug bands, early skiffle bands were novelty acts that utilized homemade instruments such as the washboard, the kazoo, and the musical saw. Due to the music's humorous, informal narrative style, skiffle is considered a precursor to rock and roll, much like rockabilly.

Alex Harvey, like Bon Scott, endured years of false starts and misplaced efforts in music before finding success with an appropriate band of younger players. After playing in the pit band of the London production of the musical *Hair,* in 1966, he began to put together a group that came into its own in 1972 as the Sensational Alex Harvey Band. His new incarnation was a rebirth, allowing Harvey to create a more theatrical, humorous, and energized stage persona. He performed with all manner of props, from canes to pirate hats, while his lead guitarist donned harlequin makeup and a one-piece spandex suit. The band lent a rougher, experimental edge to glam rock and released a series of commercially successful and critically acclaimed albums in the '70s. The band's showmanship and Harvey's visual and imaginative songwriting made their mark on Bon, but while Alex Harvey cast himself as fictional characters in songs such as "The Man in the Jar" and "The Faith Healer," Bon did not. Scott employed Harvey's similarly visual, lyrical approach and storytelling style, but had no need for fiction, since the pages of his own life were full of stories that were far stranger than any he could imagine.

These two musical influences were distilled in Bon Scott, and can be felt in every song he wrote with the Youngs. Shining examples of his unique, bawdy street balladry abound, from "T.N.T" to "Dirty Deeds (Done Dirt Cheap)" to "It's a Long Way to the Top," "Rock and Roll Singer," "Night Prowler," "Love Hungry Man," and more. All of them are written and sung from the first-person point of view of the narrator. Bon makes his statements definitively, straight from the heart and the horse's mouth. Vocally, Bon combined Jerry Lee Lewis's power with Alex Harvey's dramatic flair—but in his range and versatility, he easily and vastly surpassed them both.

"Dirty Deeds (Done Dirt Cheap)" is arguably the greatest testament to the singer's gifts and a song that features the entire scope of his voice. It is a hit-man-for-hire's ode to all those that have been done wrong, and after the song's menacing four-to-the-floor introduction, Scott starts off at the high end of his midrange as he describes the various scenarios that he can be called upon to solve. He sings the next verse more intensely, in full-voiced midrange, before he reaches the chorus, when he suddenly begins to seesaw between the upper and lower ends of his spectrum—at full volume. In the third verse, he pushes himself further, taking his voice into gritty territory without losing an ounce of clarity. Throughout, he accents his performance with bloodcurdling screams, hauntingly spoken lines, and theatrical squeals. All of these flourishes add legions to the overall tension and menace of the song, and were recorded years before the pitch-correcting recording software of today was even a pipe dream.

"When you think of Bon Scott, compared to other singers of his day, like Robert Plant, one thing to consider is how much he made out of the space he had to work with," says Professor Stewart. "Led Zeppelin began in the same kind of tradition as AC/DC, but as they went on, they really leaned more toward progressive rock, and Jimmy Page brought in a variety of influences. There was a wider space for Plant to fill musically, and he was being constantly challenged. With AC/DC, it's blues rock and so straight-ahead that the same kind of musical space wasn't there as it was in other bands at the time. Considering that fact, I think Bon Scott made a lot out of the space he was given. In 'Dirty Deeds,' he used so many parts of his voice in such a cool way—it's a real vocal showcase. It's obvious that Bon listened to a lot of blues and R & B because all of those traditions are there in his singing, but when he goes into his screeching range, he does so in a very different style. It's updated from traditional blues, but what I find most interesting is that he treats the songs the way a blues singer would. He builds them up in the same way, gaining momentum in that classic blues style as he leads the song into the title or chorus."

I never met Bon, but Brian has a fantastic personality. He is one of the great rock-and-roll front men. His stance and attitude is just to get up and do his thing and make no excuses for it. For that reason alone he should definitely be a role model for young rock-and-roll singers looking to find their way. Brian is the anti–prima donna.

—Slash

Bon Scott died at the age of thirty-three, in London, on February 19, 1980. After a night of heavy drinking at a club, he was left passed out in a car owned by an associate named Alistair Kinnear. The next evening, Kinnear found Scott's lifeless body and drove him to the hospital. He was pronounced dead on arrival and the cause of death was assumed to be pulmonary aspiration of vomit, though the official report listed two others: "acute alcohol poisoning" and "death by misadventure." Considering the time of year and the weather that night, there is a good chance that Bon was sent into hypothermic shock, and as a result, his death has remained hotly debated. In 2005, *Metal Hammer* magazine printed an exclusive interview with Alistair Kinnear, who until then had never publicly spoken of the events. His very existence and whereabouts had become such a mystery in AC/DC lore that several biographers speculated that he was no more than a ruse formulated to cover up the true cause of Bon's death, presumably from a drug overdose. The interview wasn't tremendously enlightening, but it did set the record straight. After a night of drinking, Kinnear left Bon in a car covered by a blanket with a note informing him of the address of Kinnear's flat just a few doors away. Kinnear claims that he found no vomit anywhere in the car the next day, just the singer's lifeless body under the blanket. He also reveals that a mutual friend informed him after the fact that Bon had begun treatment for acute liver damage but had skipped his doctor's appointments, and presumably his medication, that week.

In the shadow of such a fundamental loss, it is inconceivable to think that AC/DC carried on by releasing their bestselling album. It is even more inconceivable to think that they found a singer capable, not so much of filling Bon's shoes, but of replacing Bon's shoes with his own. And yet that is exactly what happened with Brian Johnson. He stepped into the recording process and put his stamp on an album that was partially written by a band whose singer, muse, and ringleader was just four months departed.

Brian Johnson grew up in Dunston, in the northeast of England, and was born just a year after Bon Scott. He came from a working-class family in a coal-mining town and learned to sing as a choirboy in his local parish. He took to singing much more so than he did to school: at fifteen he dropped out to take an apprenticeship as a fitter and turner (a kind of machinist) in a local factory, and then studied engineering at a technical college. He immediately found his way into a band with friends from work and, at their first gig, Buddy Holly's "Not Fade Away" became the first song Brian ever sang in public. Playing in bands agreed with him, and he spent every nonworking hour pursuing his pastime.

At seventeen, however, Brian joined the army and soon became a member of the Red Berets parachute regiment, with whom he went to Germany for two years. He'd always been enamored of planes and all things fast (more recently, he's made a name for himself as a race car driver), and so he relished the chance to become a paratrooper. At the end of his service, he returned home, got a job as a draftsman, and returned to rock and roll.

Throughout the '60s, Brian Johnson played in dozens of local bands in and around Newcastle, opting to make a professional go of it in 1971, with a band called USA. They ended up signing an extremely prohibitive record contract with a label called Red Bus, one that granted the label the right to change the band's name if they saw fit—which they did. Much to the dismay of their fans and the band itself, in 1972, USA became Geordie, named for the people and the impenetrable accent of their native region. They were relocated to London, where they had an even harder time getting gigs and making ends meet as a gigging band. In interviews, Johnson recalled how he and his bandmates would loiter outside of restaurants and, as patrons exited, would scurry in to grab whatever food was left on their table before it was cleared. They also resorted to getting up before dawn to steal milk as it was delivered to neighboring homes by the local milkman.

Geordie kept on and eventually enjoyed success with the release of a few singles and a subsequent appearance on *Top of the Pops,* England's equivalent of *American Bandstand,* at which point they caught the eye of the Who's Roger Daltrey. They began to open for top acts of the time such as Slade, and were supported by Supertramp at a large festival in Newcastle in 1973, which was a bit of a homecoming for them. During this time, they played two gigs with a band called Fang, featuring a salty rascal named Bon Scott. As we already know, Bon was impressed by Johnson's performance the first night he saw him—but here's why. Brian's voice was searing enough, but near the close of the set, Johnson began writhing on the floor, wailing and screaming as if possessed. Bon thought it was part of the act and was in awe; neither he nor the audience realized that the pain was real. The set was ended a few songs early, and Johnson was taken to the hospital with what he believed to be appendicitis, though it turned out to be acute food poisoning. Regardless, Bon Scott never forgot it, and when they played together again a few nights later, he was Brian's biggest fan.

After a brief peak, Geordie's popularity began to wane, as did the members' enthusiasm for the band, so they broke up in 1975. Johnson took a job repairing vinyl roofs on cars in Newcastle, but couldn't kick the urge to perform. He returned to playing rock and roll three years later, with new bandmates but the same name—Geordie. During this period, he first heard AC/DC and loved the band so much that he opted to add "Whole Lotta Rosie" to Geordie's set list. The band's regular gigs on the pub circuit were decent, but Brian wasn't satisfied, so he showed up to any professional, paying audition he happened to hear about. None of them panned out, however: he was turned down to replace Ronnie James Dio in Rainbow, and came close but missed out on joining both Uriah Heep and Manfred Mann's Earth Band.

After Bon Scott's death, Johnson's name came up in the AC/DC camp for a number of reasons. Both Young brothers had seen Geordie during a tour of Australia, and Bon had made it clear that he thought Johnson was an amazing talent. Malcolm Young had his doubts and had no interest in meeting Brian at all. He told his brothers George and Angus that he didn't think Geordie was anything to write home about, no matter what Bon had thought of Brian. Nonetheless, Brian was called down to the audition by a mutual associate, who did not tell him who the band was that he was going to jam with. As a result, upon his arrival at the rehearsal studio, Brian mistook the roadies playing pool on the first floor for the band he had turned up to meet. The roadies, in turn, took him, in his workingman's clothes, for a fellow roadie or perhaps a studio engineer on break. He was one of them, so they invited him to play a game and the lot of them shared small talk and pleasantries, no one thinking to inquire why the other was there. Thirty minutes later, someone came down from the second floor to ask if a guy named Brian Johnson had shown up—because the bastard was late.

Upstairs, Brian was welcomed with a Newcastle Brown Ale and fit right in with the band when he asked if he could smoke. After a few minutes of introductions, they got down to business: Brian was told to choose a song and immediately impressed his biggest naysayer, Malcolm, by asking if they knew Ike and Tina Turner's "Nutbush City Limits."

The song was a great choice—it's a funky, gritty blues number that allowed Brian to demonstrate his vocal range and power. They followed it up with "Whole Lotta Rosie" and a few Chuck Berry numbers, and by the end of the session, the decision, as far as the Youngs were concerned, had been made. Nonetheless, they met a few more singers, and Brian Johnson returned home to a weekend of gigs with Geordie. It took a few more rehearsals and a payout to Red Bus records, but within a month, AC/DC had a new lead singer, decidedly against all odds.

The band took off to Nassau, Bahamas, in April 1980, to begin recording at Compass Point Studios with producer Mutt Lange. To say the least it was a trial by fire for Johnson. He might have been a seasoned musician born of the rock-and-roll trenches, but he had walked into a lion's den. The Youngs possess their own musical shorthand, honed by genetics, practice, and God knows what—and Johnson, who had just met them, was required to write songs that suited their expectations, without imitating their recently departed muse. It was a Promethean task.

To make matters worse (or maybe better), the entire album had been more or less written before Bon's death—there were even titles for all the songs. Malcolm and Angus agreed that nothing could be worse than exploiting the tragedy by using the lyrics he'd been working on for the album, so they stayed true to the formula that had worked in the past and presented Brian with the music. They then awaited his words. It was hurricane season in the Bahamas when the band arrived, and the studio suffered several blackouts during the first week of their stay, leaving Brian ample time alone in his room to write, and likely to make sense of this decision he'd made. Johnson is a great storyteller and a humble narrator who is fond of relating tales where he is the punch line, the fool, or the hapless object of ridicule. As he told Tom Doyle in *Q Magazine* in 2008, during one of those stormy nights, he awoke in a cold sweat and felt as if something—or someone—otherworldly was guiding his hand. "I don't believe in God or Heaven or Hell. But something happened. We had these little rooms like cells with a bed and a toilet, no TV's. I had this big sheet of paper and I had to write some words . . . I'll never forget, I just went [*scribbles frantically as if his hand is possessed*]. I started writing and never stopped. And that was it—'Hell's Bells.' I had a bottle of whisky and I kept the light on all night, man." Whether it was the departed ghost of Bon Scott as Johnson implied, the do-or-die pressure of the situation, or the intangible synergy of meeting the right people in the right place at the right time, Johnson delivered. It wasn't the same AC/DC, but it was more than suitable to the times.

Back in Black went on to become the band's greatest bestselling album. To date, it has sold approximately 45 million copies worldwide and is the second-bestselling album of all time, after Michael Jackson's *Thriller*. With its stark black cover and funereal title, it is a fitting epitaph for Bon Scott and a statement of triumph over adversity. The album's simple, dry production also set a new benchmark in rock and roll and the science of sound engineering: studios everywhere from Norway to Nashville began to use the album as a means to test the acoustics of a room, while bands such as Motörhead used it to check their sound systems at live venues each night. The meticulous attention to detail that producer Mutt Lange, as well as Malcolm Young, brought to the recording—particularly when it came to Brian Johnson's vocals—ensured that the album set the stage for the new AC/DC. "It seemed like Bon's death spelled the demise of AC/DC," Slash says. "Replacing a singer is not easy. God knows I've been through the same thing, almost, and it's not that easy. But Brian came in and delivered two huge tracks, 'Back in Black' and 'Rock and Roll Ain't Noise Pollution,' and he set a pace for AC/DC going into the future. He and Bon are both different, obviously, but there couldn't have been a more perfect replacement singer to carry that band out for the rest of its years."

Brian Johnson's work ethic was a huge factor in setting the tone and attitude of the new band. Unlike Bon Scott, Johnson's vocal range in AC/DC is narrow. In Geordie and his other bands, Johnson had sung in a more comfortable, bluesy baritone accented with higher-register screeching. In AC/DC, however, he sings exclusively at the upper reaches of his range by sheer force of will, to the degree that every single line is delivered at the very limits of human capability.

"Bon Scott had a lot more musical range, but maybe he died before the damage was done to his instrument," Professor Stewart says. "Then again, maybe he just had strong pipes. Whatever it was, there is more variety and coloration to his voice—even his falsetto scream had variation to it.

Sometimes it was really nasal, with a really reedy sound, and sometimes it was pure and brilliant. With Brian Johnson in AC/DC, you really just get one vocal sound. It is a really great, incredible sound, but it's just the one. That is not at all a criticism, because Brian Johnson is phenomenal. For anyone to be able to sing that well with that much damage done to their vocal chords is just extraordinary."

The tonality of the new singer wasn't the only change in the band, however; Johnson was far from the larger-than-life character of his predecessor. He was an earnest, hard-working, no-nonsense front man, who would never sully Scott's memory by trying to be him on- or offstage. Rather than engage the crowd as Bon had, with between-song stories (usually about a true life misadventure from the night before) and jovial banter, Johnson took to his duties with a no-frills ethic akin to his simple workman's flat cap and jeans. AC/DC's already blistering stage show became a tighter and stronger unit as it evolved into something else on his watch. It was no longer a two-ring circus inhabited by Angus's insane performance and Bon's real-life persona. The void allowed Angus space to push his act even further, supported by Brian's steady, even-keeled presence and powerhouse delivery.

Brian's lyrical content was also a departure from AC/DC as it was. Where Bon loomed large in the songs he wrote, Brian did not and does not. His role is more of the narrative observer, making statements about the subject at hand in an impressionistic manner without necessarily following a straight narrative line. The commonalities between them, aside from an equal affinity for women and hard, fast living, are their use of the double entendre and a tongue-in-cheek sense of humor. That said, Johnson approaches lyric writing in a less poetic, more cut-and-dried, hard-edged, yet vague style. As the '70s gave way to the '80s, it was an unplanned but impeccably fitting aesthetic shift for the band. Johnson's blunt, observational, often nonlinear lyrics suited the ADD-addled, video-saturated times ahead, whereas Scott's lyrical storytelling suited a more organic, gilded age of rock and roll.

A simple example of the two singers' contrasting lyrical styles can be gleaned by listening to two songs that cover the same narrative terrain, "Shot Down in Flames" and "Shoot to Thrill." The first, from the *Highway to Hell* album, features lyrics written by Bon Scott, recounting his failed attempts at picking up women in bars. He is rejected by one that he mistakes for a prostitute, and after laying his intentions on the line with another, is turned away by her boyfriend. He is twice rebuffed, and shot down in flames. At the end of the song Bon asks Angus to shoot him down in the form of a solo, at which point he finally feels all right. In the song, Bon portrays himself as a Byronic antihero, a stance that contrasts directly with the machismo of his shrieked delivery and the song's punchy guitars. It is a nuanced, humorous, seemingly simple song that plays upon the stereotype of the ladies' man to draw the listener into the story.

"Shoot to Thrill," from *Back in Black,* is the Brian Johnson take on being a man on the prowl, and is an altogether different affair. The singer makes broad, sweeping statements, advising all women who want a "man of the street" to come to him. Rather than recount a story, he makes declarations about the women he sees, all of whom have had "too many pills." Where Bon chose humor at his own expense, Johnson takes a more traditionally macho approach, using innuendo and double entendre more directly when he sings of taking women down, firing at will, pulling the trigger, and shooting to thrill.

The differences in these two songs speak to the broader differences in the two singers and eras of AC/DC. With Bon Scott, AC/DC was a more intimate affair: there was performance synergy between Angus and the singer, to the degree that they virtually shared the front-man spotlight. Bon Scott led the audience, on record and in concert, on a journey. He was the kind of legendary character and persona that has made '70s rock classic. Brian Johnson did not—and thankfully did not try—to replicate that chemistry in the band. He brought a clean-cut blue-collar formula to AC/DC, allowing Angus to take a greater role as the symbolic leader of the band, while fulfilling his duties admirably as a singer and lyricist clearly distinct from his predecessor. As the band moved into the '80s and popular rock evolved into a harder, louder affair, Brian Johnson hit upon the perfect formula to move the band forward while honoring their past.

"It takes a tremendous physical effort to sing like Brian Johnson or Bon Scott," says Professor Stewart. "You can hear the sweat pouring down just listening to them on record. Hard rock singing like that is an athletic experience. Running around the stage is one thing; the actual singing is athletic on its own. They are both working tremendously hard. There is an extraordinary vocal control and stamina that both singers possess, and that is what distinguishes them both as superior rock singers. Few vocalists can get that sort of 'laser beam' sound in their head-voice range. To get more technical about it, both singers, but particularly Brian Johnson, are using a pure chest or speaking-range voice in what would normally be a male falsetto range. To do that with such power is incredibly difficult. In over ten years of teaching voice at Berklee, I've had just one male student be able to achieve anything close to that sound. And even that was short of the real thing."

CHAPTER THREE

BACK LINE BOOGIE

ALL MUSIC IS ABOUT RHYTHM, whether it features percussion or not, because rhythm, in its most elemental form, is a pattern of linked sounds that defines music of any kind. In human communication, rhythm is even more important—it is an essential component of how we communicate with each other, verbally or otherwise. In language, words are the vehicle, but the rhythm with which we use them is how we convey the subtleties of emotion and meaning. Take a simple phrase like "How are you?" Now think about how much can be asked with those same words depending on how they are delivered. Spoken in an even, quick rhythm, the phrase is a cursory greeting. If uttered more slowly, in a pattern that emphasizes the *are* and *you,* it's a genuine expression of concern. On an even deeper level, rhythm is how we make sense of the infinite, of what we don't understand, because it is how we measure time. Breaking time into organized, regular patterns, into variables that quantify it, allows us to measure time (and space, for that matter) and thereby somehow understand it. Rhythm is an identical form of measurement; it helps us create a beginning and an end within something that has neither, the same way that all human life begins and ends with a measured beat: the thump of the human heart is the first rhythm we ever know.

In rock and roll, the rhythm section of a band is as vital as a healthy heart and is often as overlooked. It is the muscle that brings the music to life; the pumping pulse is the tempo. Most rock, like most Western/European music of any kind, follows what is called a divisive rhythm pattern, where a four-beat measure is signified by a strong first beat and then divided into smaller sections of less-accented beats. The drummer and bass player establish this time signature and are key to keeping all the other players organized and in time. The members of the rhythm section are like contractors building a house for the rest of the band to occupy, but they do more than that—they also dictate the weather, propelling the music ahead or pulling it back via the nuances in their playing. The importance of the relationship between the bassist and the drummer cannot be overestimated when listening to rock and roll of any style or era: when the two are well matched and locked in, they anticipate each other's moves like two seasoned soccer, basketball, or hockey players. There is an intangible quality to a perfectly matched rhythm section that no technology can quite replicate and no other players can re-create. Much like a guitar player's vibrato, the way a drummer hits the drums, plus how he or she likes their skins tuned, plus how they emphasize the beats in a measure, in addition to the style of their fills within the time signature are all idiosyncratic. There are an incredible number of variables in drumming due to the mechanics of the instrument alone: essentially, drummers utilize their four limbs simultaneously, to keep time, as well as solo within the structure of the song. The sheer range of consistent, repetitive motions required over the varied surfaces of drums and cymbals, all of which can be hit with distinctive accents at any time, requires a dizzying degree of coordination. It really isn't something that anyone can just pick up without practice. Bass players have fewer variables open to them because of the nature of the instrument, but they are no less important: how hard they hit the strings, how thick their strings are, and how they choose to keep the beat when the guitar players change chords define their playing—and can greatly transform the sound of a band. A drummer and a bass player's sense of the beat when playing together really is the foundation of a rock band. Whether it is Motörhead or the Beatles, the bass and drums drive the bus, while the other elements choose the destination. Whether the bass or drums drive slightly ahead of or lag just behind the beat or tempo of the song may seem insignificant in theory, but those minor details intangibly affect the end result just as much as keeping time. I'm sorry to belabor a point, but a rhythm section in the universe of a rock song is like God, gravity, air, water, or the sun: whatever belief you're attuned to, it's the element nothing else can exist without. And there's really no two ways about it: a good rhythm section makes a band better. It's almost their reason for being—it provides the magnetic pull that keeps the other moving parts in orbit.

AC/DC probably have one of the best rhythm sections of all time. The only time that AC/DC ever sucked was during the period when Phil Rudd left the band. He is the perfect fit for the AC/DC sound.

—Slash

Philip Hugh Norman Witschke Redzevcuts, born in Melbourne in 1954, is the only long-standing member of AC/DC to be born in Australia. He started to play drums in high school, though his family neither supported nor encouraged it. Phil dropped out of school at fifteen, began an apprenticeship with an electrician, and, once he'd earned some money, bought himself a drum kit. He says that he took exactly one formal lesson, opting instead to play along to recordings of his heroes and learn on the fly, sitting close enough to his speakers that he could hear the records over the sound of his own drums. His "teachers" were all classic, solid stylists: Simon Kirke of Free and Bad Company, Corky Laing of Mountain, Ringo Starr of the Beatles, and Kenny Jones of the Small Faces.

It didn't take him long to start playing in local bands. In 1972, he joined Mad Mole, a band that played by-the-numbers blues rock, as well as Krayne, a more progressive trio closer in spirit to Uriah Heep and Deep Purple that featured a friend of his from school, Geordie Leach, on bass. Rudd left both bands to join Charlemagne who stayed together about a year and played nothing but Humble Pie, Small Faces, and Free covers in bars and at parties. In 1973, Rudd and Geordie Leach resumed playing together and got more serious about their endeavors. They dubbed their new band Smack, and after rehearsing together for a few weeks they began inviting singers to join them. They found their front man the moment Gary "Angry" Anderson walked in, and they signed him up on the spot. Anderson's raspy voice and tough-as-nails persona are legendary in Australian rock: he and Leach would later form the iconic Aussie band Rose Tattoo, of whom AC/DC were early supporters. From 1978 through 1984, Rose Tattoo's first four albums were produced by George Young and Harry Vanda, and, though they were never widely embraced in the United States, they were a tremendous influence on the nascent L.A. metal scene that spawned Mötley Crüe, Guns N' Roses, Faster Pussycat, Ratt, and many more. "Rose Tattoo was great when they played here in L.A. in the early '80s—just totally kick-ass, wearing all this leather," says Tommy Lee, drummer for Mötley Crüe. "Angry Anderson was the first guy that we ever saw who had full sleeve tattoos like that."

But first came Smack, who assiduously renamed themselves Buster Brown and set about playing bars, covering the Rolling Stones, the Faces, Elton John, Stevie Wonder, Eric Clapton, and everyone else with a hard blues backbeat. They got onto the bill at the Sunbury Pop Festival in 1974, an outdoor event that boasted an attendance of thirty thousand people, and went over so well that the crowd called them back for two encores. Buster Brown became busy enough in the wake of that show that Rudd was forced to quit his day job. The band got a record deal and recorded an album, but the fact that they were making next to no money became a point of contention for Rudd—who complained so loudly that the other members fired him.

Rudd spent most of the next year working at his father's used car dealership until a mutual friend told him that AC/DC was looking for a drummer and bassist. Rudd asked Geordie Leach to join him at the audition, but Leach refused, so Rudd showed up alone at the house that the Youngs and Bon Scott shared, trying out in their hallway "rehearsal room." He was greeted there by the band members wearing nothing but their underwear, partly because of the heat but mostly to intimidate the musicians they were auditioning that day. Rudd stayed as cool as possible as he ran through material from the band's upcoming album, *High Voltage,* as well as blues and rock classics they all knew. He proved to them quickly that he had the skills to man the fills.

Phil Rudd was as instantaneous a fit for the band as Bon Scott had been. He provided a steady backbeat, with an almost inhuman precision but just enough flair to drive the rest of the band. He was the rock they needed. Finding the proper bass player wouldn't prove as easy. The band had already run through a succession of them, including their only American member, their first bassist, Larry Von Kriedt. When Phil joined the band, Malcolm and George Young were splitting bass duties out of necessity—Malcolm on records, when George was behind the production board, and George onstage. Every party involved hoped Geordie Leach would come along with Rudd, but after Leach refused the gig again (after another invitation), George Young approached another noted player, Lobby Loyde, the guitarist for the Coloured Balls, a band who, along with the MC5, the Flamin' Groovies, and the Stooges, paved the way for punk rock. Playing with AC/DC would be a change of pace for Loyde, yet one he could handle. He seriously considered the offer, mostly because for a short time Rudd had played in the Coloured Balls. Loyde knew firsthand how well Phil Rudd could lock down and swing a rock-and-roll beat.

The quest for a bassist went on, well into early 1975, after the release of their debut album, until they found one courtesy of Steve McGrath, one of their roadies. He made one mistake, however, in telling his friend Mark Evans (who, luckily, played both bass and guitar proficiently) that AC/DC needed an additional *guitar* player. He got Evans an audition, and his friend learned the songs on *High Voltage* overnight, only to discover when he arrived that the band expected him to play them on bass. Evans was just eighteen and had only been playing bass for about a year, but he was skilled enough that he got the job. His hiring seems to have been two parts skill to two parts necessity: the band were so sick of not having a regular player that they would accept one who was committed that they could teach rather than search further for one with experience. They hired Evans, probably thinking it would be just for a few months. To wit: Evans didn't even meet Bon until his first gig with the band a week later. It was a memorable meeting, however: Evans had previously been banned from the venue for fighting with a bouncer, so when he was refused entry, only Bon's salty charm could rectify the situation and ensure that the show would go on at all.

Mark Evans played on the international release of *High*

Voltage ("Can I Sit Next to You Girl" was rerecorded), "T.N.T," "Dirty Deeds (Done Dirt Cheap)," and "Let There Be Rock." He can be seen in the promotional videos for "Jailbreak" and "It's a Long Way to the Top (If You Wanna Rock and Roll)"—but his tenure lasted only until 1977, when he was fired during a European tour over differences with Angus Young. Neither Evans nor either of the Young brothers have ever explained the roots of the tension or gone into detail about how Evans was let go. Angus later said that Evans didn't have the backbone for a life in the music business— essentially, that he was too nice to stick with the band. Evans has said only that it was the best decision for both parties. The truth most likely lies in the middle.

When Evans was fired, the band was on the verge of an important tour of America, so a replacement had to be found immediately. The band's manager at the time, Michael Browning, suggested an Englishman from Liverpool named Cliff Williams. Born in 1949, he was a bit older than Rudd and the Youngs, and wasn't really a fan of the band. Browning was convinced that Williams, in personality and playing, was the man, however, and persisted to the point of coaching and coaxing. He set up the audition and, in the days leading up to it, pretty much told Williams what to play. Browning was trying to nip what he saw as a problem in the bud: the Youngs were dead set on hiring Colin Pattenden from Manfred Mann's Earth Band—who was significantly older. He could have played the tunes well enough, but visually his gray hair would have stuck out like a sore thumb. Browning's machinations were well intended and completely correct, because after just one rehearsal, Williams, with his easygoing personality and workingman's attitude, fell in naturally with the rest of the brood.

Williams's story was different, but essentially he was of the same stock as the other members. He had started playing guitar at ten, and just two years later he was proficient enough to play with cover bands in clubs and pubs. At fourteen, he switched to bass to fill a vacancy and earn his keep in a local group with regular gigs. By sixteen he had left school to work in a factory, but his passion for music soon took precedence over the regulated workingman's life: he quit to play music full-time and enjoyed short-lived success in the form of a string of regular gigs with a local band. Williams was a teenager, and I'm sure he thought he'd made it—until his band's singer was sacked by the other players and the group fell apart. Williams did what any sensible youth with a dream would: he headed for London to pursue his destiny. There he found his path much tougher than expected. He was soon penniless and unemployed and even homeless for a time. He regrouped and eventually worked with a few blues bands while holding down a number of jobs, in a supermarket, in a machine shop, and doing demolition for a contractor.

In 1970, a bit older and wiser, Williams placed an ad in a music paper and met guitarist Laurie Wisefield, with whom he formed two progressive rock bands, Sugar and then Home, both critically acclaimed and successful. The UK's *Melody Maker* called Home's eponymous second album one of the best of 1972, and the band landed gigs opening for Led Zeppelin, Slade, Mott the Hoople, and others. Every review of the band's live show mentioned that on several numbers, Williams played bass with a violin bow. Home split up in 1974, when Wisefield joined Wishbone Ash, and after that Williams worked his way through a few short-lived bands, none promising. The phone call from Michael Browning was just the regular gig Williams was after, even though he cared little for the band he was about to join.

[One] thing that separates AC/DC as a hard-rock band is that you can dance to their music. They didn't play funk, but everything they played was funky. And that beat could really get a crowd going.

—Rick Rubin, producer

Mark Evans's playing in AC/DC was solid, and his contribution to the band's momentous early albums cannot be denied. He and Phil Rudd created the propulsive foundation that allowed the Youngs and Bon Scott to shine. But once Cliff Williams entered the picture, the rhythm section went from black-and-white to Technicolor. Williams and Rudd are as perfectly matched as Angus and Malcolm. They are an impenetrable pair that swings in a very simple, primal, inimitable way.

"Cliff and Phil work as if they're a machine," Slash says. "But unlike machines, their rhythms have a very human feel. They synch together really, really well. They create a rhythm that just makes you *feel* something. One of the signature things about AC/DC is that they've got this uncompromising and unforgiving signature swagger, and a huge part of that is the rhythm section. It can be imitated, but no one can touch it. It's a very sleazy kind of sound that's very tough, and it's all part of the chemistry between those guys, but it's led heavily by the rhythm section, as simple as it is."

Williams never plays much more than a succession of eighth notes in the root note of the song, a pattern that can be found in Chapter One of any bass-playing manual. Elevating such a basic form, giving it a feel, a tone, and a presence, is something else entirely. Song after song, Williams lends the music a funk that isn't typical of hard rock music. On paper, his parts are mechanical: he's often playing the same note repeatedly with few or no chord changes. It may sound like a contradiction, but it's clear that Williams is skilled at his craft and capable of more complicated playing *because* of the simplicity of what he does within AC/DC. It is the fact that he plays the same bass line *without* sounding robotic that makes him exceptional. Cliff achieves a deep, resounding tone by using thick strings on his bass and plucking the strings hard, instinctually laying his lines just a touch ahead of the drums at all times. He is the driving force that keeps the music on edge. He and Rudd create a locomotive strut that is the core of AC/DC. It's much more nuanced and vibrant than the hammering beats of classic or alternative rock because there is an uncharacteristic swing there, with one foot in funk and the other in the blues.

Every song in the AC/DC catalog is more or less defined by that rhythm section, but *Powerage* and *Highway to Hell* are two albums that really showcase the band's superior back line. In songs such as "Rock and Roll Damnation," "Riff Raff," "Highway to Hell," "Girls Got Rhythm," and "Love Hungry Man," are prime examples of a top-notch drum and bass player leading a powerhouse band. Rudd's and Williams's playing is markedly tighter, and that infuses the music with a more muscular quality. The push and pull between the rhythm and the guitars and vocals is markedly more dynamic on these albums—and their vigorous tension is undeniable.

"AC/DC have such a cool groove," says Robin Stone, associate professor of guitar at the Berklee College of Music. "They're almost like two different bands because the rhythm section has that real seventies rock sound. They're very analog, very warm, very indicative of the groove-oriented dance-rock that was going on in the mid-seventies. And then there is Angus and Malcolm, who have that, too, but they're a bit of a separate faction. They bring the straight-ahead hard rock and blues edge. But the rhythm section makes it all very danceable because it's got such a nice groove. I never truly appreciated Cliff Williams's and Phil Rudd's playing until I saw them play live. Then I started listening more intently to the whole picture of what the band was doing, rather than just the guitars. Their rhythm section doesn't get any notoriety at all, but they should because Phil Rudd especially is just warm, not jazzed out, and has a great feel."

Sometimes only the absence of something can make its

value truly understood, as was the case when Phil Rudd left the band from 1983 through 1993. Following the gargantuan international success of *Back in Black* and their first American number one with *For Those About to Rock,* the band reconvened, after years of nonstop touring, to write what Malcolm Young intended to be a more stripped-down, less produced album than the previous two. He wanted the band to sound like they did in the beginning—in essence returning to their roots now that they'd grown comfortable with their new singer. They returned to Compass Point Studios in Nassau, Bahamas, where they'd recorded *Back in Black,* to begin the process. Rudd arrived and laid down his tracks for the album with characteristic perfection, but they would be the last he'd play with the band for the next decade.

Rudd has said in interviews that Bon Scott's death hit him very hard, much harder than it hit any of the others. The fact that they'd recorded and toured nonstop following his death wore on him, and he filled the void with alcohol and drugs. Years later, Angus said that they were worried that Phil would have gone overboard and hurt himself or others had he embarked on another world tour. It didn't help matters that what biographers have referred to only vaguely as a "messy personal situation" between Rudd and a member of the Youngs' circle had sparked a growing tension between him and Malcolm that erupted into a booze-addled altercation in the studio. Malcolm, who was quite the drinker at the time, arranged to have Rudd fired and flown home on the next plane.

For the next ten years, AC/DC was not the same. Their next five albums were uneven, containing one or two stand-out tracks, a few duds, and too many songs that were passable yet uninspired for a band with such a rich history of riffs. Replacement drummer Simon Wright kept time well enough, but he lacked the chemistry with Cliff Williams that Phil Rudd had. His replacement, Chris Slade, who had played with everyone from Manfred Mann to Paul Rodgers and the Firm to David Gilmour of Pink Floyd, proved a more inspired choice. With Chris Slade behind the drum kit, the band recorded *The Razor's Edge* and regained their footing: buoyed by such tracks as "Thunderstruck" and "Money Talks," the album hit the top of the charts in the U.S. and UK and was a return to form in every way.

Rudd had spent his time away from the band in New Zealand, where he moved immediately after being sacked to avoid the unwanted attention he was sure to get in Australia. He had always been a man of ever-changing hobbies, which he indulged to the fullest in his decade away. His earliest was recording his experiences with a video camera, which he'd begun to do while the band was on tour back in the '70s. He then added model airplane building to his repertoire: when the band moved out of a rented house back in the early days, the landlord was sure to find, among more chaotic and less hygienic debris, a finely detailed model airplane. Rudd later turned to sailing toy boats, and soon elevated his love of driving fast to proper auto racing. The need for speed had always been with him: back when the band was touring the Australian countryside by van, they appointed

Phil their getaway driver on those (too frequent) occasions when they were chased out of town, usually by an angry father or boyfriend looking for Bon.

In New Zealand, during his hiatus, Rudd did not play drums for six straight years. He bought a helicopter charter company that gave aerial tours of the stunning countryside and further indulged his love of competitive auto racing. Rudd also won a few handgun marksmanship competitions and even (according to his own account) planted crops and farmed. After a few years, however, he returned to music by building a working studio, in which he began to play drums again when he wasn't serving as a producer and recording engineer for local bands. That taste of the music world was enough to lead him back to the fold when Malcolm invited him to jam with the band in London. Once he did, Malcolm realized that no premeditated, stripped-down recording technique in the world could get AC/DC back to their original sound better than reuniting them with the missing piece of the puzzle.

"I got the chance to work with AC/DC on the 1995 album, *Ballbreaker*," producer Rick Rubin told *Rolling Stone* in 2004. "The best thing was the return of Phil Rudd, who had left the band in 1982. To me, that made them AC/DC again. You can hear it in how he drags behind the beat. It's that same rhythm that first drew me to them in junior high."

Ballbreaker would be the band's only collaboration with Rubin, whose work habits—demanding upward of forty takes on some songs, not being present every day in the studio—did not gel with Malcolm's intensely focused approach to recording. But the album was well received, and the return of the rhythm section had fans rejoicing. The backbone of the band was once again intact, and the tours supporting *Ballbreaker* and the next album, *Stiff Upper Lip,* were as powerful as any they'd ever done. No matter how skilled the replacement drummers had been, no one ever sounded quite like Phil Rudd does counting off the start to "Back in Black"— and no one ever will.

"I was so happy to see Phil back in the band," Tommy Lee says. "I can count my inspirations on one hand when it comes to the players I listened to growing up and he is one of them. His drums always sounded cool, plus he was the master of simplicity. Just every once in a while he'll hit a crash cymbal or something, but other than that he does what a drummer has to do—he fucking holds it *down*! He is the king of the two and four beat. If you want to hear a drummer locking everything into place, time after time, it doesn't get any better. He's four on the floor and I fucking love it. My style as a drummer is definitely different, but when I'm tracking songs for an album and doing my basic drum tracks, I think about Phil's playing to keep what I'm doing super simple, super solid, and sounding really cool and really great. I learned a lot, simplicity-wise, from him. He taught me when to pour it on and when to do absolutely the bare minimum so you can listen to the lyrics and really hear what the guitars are doing. His beat is what everyone is pounding their feet and pumping their fists in the air to! That beat makes the entire stadium move. You can never underestimate how important that is to the entire band's sound."

In AC/DC, nothing is ever quite as simple as it seems, however. There is an almost invisible complexity to the music that is unanimously felt but singularly understood. The rhythm and root of the band is no different. As much as the bass and drums exist as a perfect entity, they almost have no meaning without an essential third element: the rhythm guitar playing of Malcolm Young. In most rock bands, from the Rolling Stones to Radiohead to U2 and on down the line, the rhythm guitarist is a foil for the lead guitarist. The two exist in their own world, usually atop the rhythm section, if music can be thought of in two dimensions, dictating the chord changes and emotional shifts in the song. In AC/DC, that's not the case. In AC/DC, rhythm guitarist Malcolm Young plays two roles at once—in just about every song. He is the driving force in the songwriting, and his playing is the rock off of which his brother Angus solos into the sky. But Malcolm's parts in every AC/DC song are much more important than that, because without them there would be nothing. Malcolm is the invisible member of the rhythm section; he is the one who puts the timekeeping in context. He is the secret weapon that would be impossible to replace.

"One thing that Malcolm doesn't do is play a lot of notes," says J3, a seasoned guitarist who has toured with Sevendust and recorded with Tommy Lee. "The way he does rhythm guitar is to play very few notes in exactly the right spot all the time, exactly the way a great bass player does. He lives in that behind-the-beat kind of feel, but instead of playing rhythm guitar patterns, he's dropping just one chord in there. And it's always in the right spot, the same way John Bonham had that behind-the-beat groove playing drums in Led Zeppelin. That's how Malcolm plays guitar. Put it this way. If you take his guitar out of any of their songs, from 'Girls Got Rhythm' to 'Back in Black,' you are looking at very simple rhythm playing. The drums are almost machine-perfect and so is the bass. There's a groove, but there's not too much swing. Think about 'Back in Black': the beat is just boom-cha, boom-cha. Now add Malcolm's rhythm line. Uhn-uhn-nuh-unuh . . . You hear that? It's his playing that makes 'Back in Black' a dance song."

CHAPTER FOUR

DEATH BEFORE COMPROMISE

THERE ARE FEW BANDS

in the history of rock and roll that knew who they were and sounded how they sounded, literally, from their very first record. The Beatles' early recordings are incredible, but their youthful energy on *Please Please Me* is a far cry from *Revolver* or *Let It Be*. The Rolling Stones' earliest albums are stylish, well-executed '60s white-boy blues, but they're miles from the rich, dynamic, expansive playing of *Let It Bleed* and *Sticky Fingers*. The same goes for Led Zeppelin, the Who, the Kinks, and just about every other pillar of classic rock and roll. AC/DC is the rare exception. Despite the youth of Angus and Malcolm Young, and despite the band's roster changes, AC/DC's first record is an exact blueprint of their sound as it remains to this day. The pair knew what they wanted to be and knew how they wanted to do it from the very beginning. It didn't matter to them that the music they wanted to do in 1973 was hardly the sound of the day. 1973, that was the year of the release of Pink Floyd's prog-rock masterpiece *Dark Side of the Moon*, David Bowie's *Alladin Sane*, the Rolling Stones' *Goat's Head Soup*, Led Zeppelin's *Houses of the Holy*, Wings' *Band on the Run*, Elton John's *Goodbye Yellow Brick Road*, and the Who's *Quadrophenia*. Aside from the Stooges' *Raw Power*, there wasn't a heaping helping of straight-ahead, overamplified rock and roll being released by any major acts who mattered worldwide.

AC/DC were as wonderfully alien to the sound of the day as they were a completely formed entity when they arrived. Their first four albums aren't shaky or uneven; they're not the sound of musicians finding their way. They are complete, undeniable statements; they are the realization of a musical language and a rock-and-roll vision that burst full-blown from the Young brothers, seemingly since the moment they first picked up guitars. The pair may not even have been aware of it; in fact, their attitude about their music has always been "It's just what we do"; but to know what to do without a period of experimentation is extraordinary. It took the band, as it would any band, a few albums to reach their creative peak, but by 1979, they were into recording their seminal albums—*Highway to Hell, Back in Black,* and *For Those About to Rock (We Salute You)*—all of which are distinguished more by Robert "Mutt" Lange's immaculate production than by any musical departure from their earliest recordings. Lange's studio direction highlighted the band's strengths as they'd never been captured before, and by the time they hit that stride their playing and songwriting had been polished by years of touring experience, so musically, nothing was all that different from the songs on *High Voltage* or *Dirty Deeds Done Dirt Cheap*.

That's not to say that AC/DC never got better. The point is that they were *always that good*.

To know who you are and what you want to be from the start, for an artist of any kind, is incredibly freeing. It has allowed AC/DC a focus that has bucked thirty years of trends. If you look at their entire career, most would agree that they hit a creative low point in the late '80s, with less successful albums such as *Flick of the Switch* and *Fly on the Wall,* but regardless, AC/DC never made the mistake that so many other established bands did in that decade. It would have been blasphemous and disastrous if they had, say, experimented with keyboards like Van Halen or otherwise altered their sound to suit the trends. It should be noted that there are also no photos of AC/DC in bad '80s attire and that their only nod to the video star era was the extremely loose "concept" (if you can call it that) performance video that accompanied the release of *Fly on the Wall*.

How did AC/DC manage to avoid the uncharacteristic choices that led other established bands off track once MTV made visual consumption of music the new norm? By resolutely opting not to be a product of the times, come what may. Rather than scramble to find their place in the new musical landscape, AC/DC remained absolutely themselves, even if it meant coming off like dinosaurs to some.

"When you look at AC/DC's catalog, they just always had it down," says J3, a guitarist who has toured with Sevendust and Tommy Lee. "The nuts and bolts of the band's sound were there from Day 1, 1973. And if you think about what people were doing at the time, they *weren't* doing it. It's as if they grew up and that's just the way they were. They've had the same look and sound since 1973, too. As steady as the beat is in their music, so was their resolve to be exactly who they are. They weren't going to change for anything— not for marketing, not for trends. They weren't going to change the style of music or try drum machines just because that was what other people were doing. They are one of those bands that live outside of the bubble, like Pantera or Iron Maiden or U2 to a large degree. It doesn't matter what anybody else is doing, they're just going to do what they do."

They may have ignored the '80s, following no other leader but themselves, but whether they cared or not, AC/DC's three most successful albums redefined what modern hard rock could sound like—and the level of commercial success it could reach in that decade. Unlike progressive acts or harder, faster metal bands, AC/DC employed a simple, primal groove that made hard-edged rock danceable, and those three albums deftly captured that essence of their music. That trio of albums literally opened the doors for so many bands that followed as the '80s wore on.

Malcolm Young had always been a stickler for simple production and for capturing AC/DC as they sounded when they played the songs all together in the same room, live in the studio. He and Angus never regarded the studio as another instrument or as a tool to lend the music a dimension that was not there. What AC/DC did so well with producer Mutt Lange on *Highway to Hell* was to capture the sound in Malcolm's head by creating a very dry, in-your-face ambience devoid of unnecessary effects. Once again, their approach was out of time. In 1979, all the big rock bands from Led Zeppelin to Black Sabbath to the Who were doing what they could in the studio to create vast, echoing, tangible moodiness on tape—because back then the only option was capturing music on two-inch-thick tape. AC/DC turned away from all that, very clearly separating themselves from the pack yet again. Rather than striving for false grandeur on their LPs, they strove to bring their listeners front and center so they could overpower them with their playing. During the recording of *Back in Black,* engineer Tony Platt, who'd worked on *Highway to Hell,* had to re-create that mood in a completely different studio, since Malcolm and Mutt Lange both agreed that if anything the new album must go further in that direction production-wise. Luckily, Platt had some ideas. He recorded several tracks of room ambience—literally, microphones recording the sound of the silent room that the band would be recorded in at Compass Point Studios—that he layered beneath their performance tracks in the final mix, thus creating a sonic facsimile of the actual room to surround the playing recorded in it. The result brings the listener closer to the music, giving them a true sense of what it was like to be in the room when the songs were captured. Don't take it from me, try it out for yourself: put on a pair of headphones and cue up the song "Back in Black." It's not a new recording, and it was done well before digital became the norm, but I'll be damned if I don't feel like I'm underneath the hi-hat when Phil Rudd starts counting it off. If *Highway to Hell* represents AC/DC at their purest, *Back in Black* is the tour de force.

"*Highway to Hell* is probably the most natural-sounding rock record I've ever heard," multi-Grammy-winning producer Rick Rubin told *Rolling Stone* in 2004. "There's so little adornment. Nothing gets in the way of the push and pull between the guitarists, the bassist and the drummer. For me, it's the embodiment of rock-and-roll. When I'm producing a rock band I try to create albums that sound as powerful as *Highway to Hell*. Whether it's the Cult or the Red Hot Chili Peppers, I apply the same basic formula: keep it sparse. Make the guitar parts more rhythmic. It sounds simple, but what AC/DC did is almost impossible to duplicate. A great band like Metallica could play an AC/DC song note for note and they still wouldn't capture the tension and release that drives the music. There's nothing like it."

As the icons of the '60s and '70s set off on artistic side roads at the dawn of the '80s, AC/DC made their ultimate statement. And as the decade wore on and got stranger, that statement was heard loud and clear. As the Stones donned Technicolor spandex, released solo albums, and covered Motown songs, and, in the wake of Led Zeppelin, Robert Plant turned to '50s-style pop crooning (with the Honeydrippers), while Van Halen changed their sound and Ozzy Osbourne wrote ballads and hair metal came into vogue, AC/DC remained the same. They didn't need to worry about fitting in because they'd already carved out their niche. "Particularly in the eighties, older bands felt like they had to reinvent themselves to stay current and find a spot in the culture of the day," J3 says. "But AC/DC just didn't care. They made their seminal records—*Highway to Hell, Back in Black,* and *For Those About to Rock*—in an amazing three-year stretch from 1979 to 1981, before the eighties even got its pants on. And the funny thing is that, even though it was ten years later, and they were still so separate from the sound of the day, they actually somehow *defined* the sound of the eighties. They were really ahead of the curve with those three records because they opened the door for a ton of bands that didn't get on the charts until years later. Put it this way, if it weren't for the success of *Back in Black* at commercial radio, it would have been much tougher for harder-sounding bands like Mötley Crüe and Guns N' Roses to get airplay when they came along."

The end of the '80s was a creative downtime for AC/DC, but when alternative rock pushed bands like Def Leppard off the charts and out of style, it didn't affect AC/DC at all. Similarly, the mixed bag of grunge, rap rock, and all things '90s did little to put a dent in AC/DC's record sales: their entire back catalog continued to go multiplatinum in America throughout the decade, even as bands from Nirvana and Pearl Jam to Korn and Limp Bizkit had their moments at the top of the charts. Again, AC/DC succeeded through an uncompromising devotion to their original vision.

In the 2000s, AC/DC returned to top form by reuniting their original lineup. The old adage of not fixing what isn't broken very much applied to AC/DC. Once the original lineup was again in place, everything clicked for them again and a mainstream renaissance was soon at hand for the band. Sounding better than ever, they mounted a giant tour for *Stiff Upper Lip* that involved more than fifty tons of gear, seventeen semi trucks, and a thirty-foot-tall, three-ton statue of Angus that blew smoke and grew horns. The scale of the tour—and the ticket sales—caught the eye of the media as the band continued to attract new, ever younger fans.

AC/DC's recent eight-year break, during which they

scrapped an almost completed album and began again with a new producer, did nothing but whet the public's appetite for new music and some live dates. Promoters worldwide had offered the band millions to do a string of shows, or even a one-off gig, but AC/DC stuck to their guns, as they always had, and never capitalized on an opportunity to tour without an album to promote. They simply disappeared back into their lives until they were ready, even refusing to play at the Sydney Olympics in 2000 because they were asked to lip-synch. "We heard that they wanted us to mime and stuff," Angus told Melbourne's *Sunday Herald Sun*. "There are some things in life that just don't mix. And to me, sport and music are completely different animals."

As obvious yet overlooked as that statement is, so, too, is the fact that the band has remained true to the values of '70s rock, despite drastic changes in the music industry. In the '70s, the album was king. An LP record was seen as a statement and a snapshot of a period of time in a band's career. It was something to be heard start to finish and consumed as a whole, not in pieces. Back when record stores and mail-order catalogs were the only ways for music fans to buy records and tapes, and music magazines and a handful of television shows were the only media outlets devoted to reporting on music, being a fan required more effort. There was no readily accessible network aside from friends and fellow fans; there were no Twitter updates. An album release by a major band was an *event,* and a concert was a gathering of the fellow faithful. A new album was something that fans pored over, talked about, and couldn't wait to see performed live. An album became an entity that inhabited a period of time in the minds of music consumers; albums, as a whole, were the soundtracks of their memories.

Today, that magic and mystery—and the anticipation for a band to return to be consumed—are gone for the most part in modern musical culture. The commodity of singles—experiencing just one song from an artist—not too long ago wasn't the prevalent norm across all genres of music the way it is today. The ability to log on to the iTunes Store, Rhapsody, Limewire, and other online vendors to instantly download a track has transformed how the public will consume music forever. Technology has also eliminated the mystery necessitated by distance: MySpace, Facebook, and Twitter grant today's music fans constant access to their favorite bands if they so choose. Cable television, the Internet, numerous late-night talk shows in need of musical guests, as well as advertisements and youth-oriented reality and scripted television shows, provide endless opportunities for musical artists to expose themselves to the public. Technology has even opened the door for artists to instantly release music directly to their fans if they choose to. In short, the pace of supply and consumption has sped up as a result of the increase in available outlets. And as a result, so have the life cycles of new artists.

This is a modern revolution that the pillars of classic rock have all joined once it proved to be a viable commercial outlet for their back catalogs—all of them except AC/DC. They are the only ones who remain steadfast in their commitment to selling nothing but their albums in their entirety, in any format, to the public, as they've always done. To this day, they have never released a proper single-disc Greatest Hits compilation (though 1986's *Who Made Who* came close, collecting a few hits, some deep album cuts, and one brand-new title track). True to form, all of AC/DC's compilations feature rarities of one type or another, making each one collectible in its own right. They have also been very frank about their reluctance to make their music available digitally. It has nothing to do with the medium itself, just that until Apple allows artists to sell albums in their entirety in the iTunes Store, AC/DC will not participate.

At a time when CD sales continue to drop and music retail institutions such as Tower Records and the Virgin Megastores have closed up shop, I would expect any band, particularly one made up of guys in their late fifties and early sixties returning from an eight-year hiatus, to embrace every outlet available to them to release their music both new and old. No one in AC/DC is getting any younger, and it's likely that *Black Ice* will be their last hurrah, so ignoring the digital domain, from a business standpoint, seemed headstrong and ill advised. But the band went beyond denying digital download sales with their latest release—they even rejected what remains of traditional record distribution, opting to make the album available only at Wal-Mart stores, Sam's Clubs, or via their Web site. It seemed like image suicide, aligning with Wal-Mart, a decidedly mainstream chain known for censoring its inventory. If anything, it was anticredible—because it certainly wasn't "cool." But it wasn't stupid, either: in the vast expanses of rural America, unfortunately, Wal-Mart has become the only guarantee because in many locales it's the only game in town. To a band that never cared to be cool, the choice to have the album available everywhere on the same day, regardless of the venue, made sense.

The only nod that AC/DC has made to the way that younger generations consume music was their decision to license their music to the company that produces the wildly popular video game *Rock Band*. But again, rather than license a few songs, they insisted that their entire *Live at Donington* album be transposed into the game's play-along interface so that fans could experience the band as they're meant to be—live. To date, they have no plans to make any singles available for download for the game. It is yet another example of the band doing nothing other than what they see fit to do, remaining utterly themselves and completely true to form.

The band's retail plans for *Black Ice* were announced months before the release of the album in October 2008—and were received, by the press at least, with skepticism. That quickly turned to praise once the album's sales worldwide became proof positive that the public didn't hold AC/DC's multimillion-dollar Wal-Mart deal against them. *Black Ice* debuted at number one in twenty-nine countries around the world and sold approximately 5 million copies internationally in its first week. In the United States it racked up the biggest first-week sales by a hard rock band since Sound-Scan started tracking them in 1991. And, perhaps more astonishingly, it became only AC/DC's second U.S. number one (after *For Those About to Rock* in 1981). The subsequent

Rock 'N Roll Train tour was the highest grossing rock-and-roll tour of the year.

AC/DC has existed at the center of its own self-established world, defiant of and generally ignored by critics, while both their music and their image withstood the test of time. As they've kept the music pristine and powerful, their workingman's clothes and timeless outlaw rock-and-roll style have never grown old: just as trendy clothes don't typically age well, blue jeans only get better. But . . . while their image has remained basically the same, the band has always enjoyed toying with it. Bon Scott was a huge fan of Frank Zappa, whose anticommercial criticism of the music industry and artsy image manipulation took Bob Dylan's *Don't Look Back*—era assault on the press into a new decade. In the early days, as AC/DC toured the byways of Australia taking any gig they could get, they were frequently booked into gay clubs that mistook their name for a nod to bisexuality. Undeterred by the misunderstanding, the undeniably heterosexual singer would respond by playing to the crowd and turning up his onstage seduction to eleven. In the same vein, Scott made the band's first appearance on Australian national television memorable by appearing in drag on *Countdown with Molly Meldrum* in 1975. He told none of his bandmates, arriving just before showtime dressed as the schoolgirl counterpart to Angus's schoolboy and serenading him as they ran through their cover of Big Joe Williams's "Baby, Please Don't Go."

Bon Scott embodied the band in so many ways, but when they lost him, rather than find another singer who lived and breathed the rock-and-roll life the way he did, they found one who delivered musically and allowed that singer to write lyrics that reflected *his* perspective. Faced with a loss that would have caused most bands to lose their footing, give up, or at least change their style, AC/DC did none of it. They managed to integrate Brian Johnson into the band by letting him be himself—within months of losing Bon. "There are two different AC/DCs," J3 says. "The Bon Scott version was more lyrically honest. I bought it, I really believed him. He just wanted to drink himself into the floor, fuck your girlfriend, and shoot somebody—and in the songs he's telling you that. That's not to say Brian Johnson doesn't mean what he's singing, but Bon was the guy who really was going to leave the show and go and do all of those things he said he was going to do. Brian is the guy who is going to a bar somewhere. But that's a good place for him to be coming from lyrically because it's much more honest. If they had tried to replace Bon, who was *the guy,* with someone trying to come off like Bon did, it would never have worked and they would have lost a lot of fans. Because finding another Bon? Impossible. That was never going to happen."

The key to AC/DC's authenticity and integrity has always been their unwillingness to compromise their concept of what and who they are. They have never felt the need to prove themselves or expand their musical legacy beyond the simple truth and power of their live performance. They've also avoided the limelight that every rock star large and small seems to crave as much as they do a multimillion-dollar record deal. They let the music do the talking and let nothing else get in the way. "I say all the time that we're like a thrash version of AC/DC," guitarist Kerry King of Slayer says. "That's certainly not a shot at AC/DC because I think Slayer is a good band. What I mean is that what we've done historically is similar to what they've done—we are who we are and that's that. Once you establish yourself as doing something, that's what fans like you to do. You can name shitloads of bands who have made drastic left turns in their careers and left most of their audience behind. I'm a fan of both Slayer and AC/DC and I can say, as a fan, that both of them have remained completely true to their sound."

AC/DC hasn't drifted anywhere, ever. This is what they do, this is what you get, this is AC/DC. You have to give them props for that. This band has been around since the early seventies and they have more fans than ever today. When music is constantly changing these days, for them to just go, "You know what? Fuck that, we're doing this," that's pretty fucking ballsy.

—Tommy Lee

In 2008, for the first time in thirty-five years, however, AC/DC was a darling of the critics. They'd never before been widely praised by the music press that "mattered." Remember that 1976 *Rolling Stone* review of *High Voltage*? In 1976, as mentioned earlier in this book, the magazine was dismissive at best, citing guitars, bass, and drums that all "goose-step together in mindless three-chord formations," while "Lead singer Bon Scott spits out his vocals with a truly annoying aggression, which I suppose is the only way to do it when all you seem to care about is being a star so that you can get laid every night." Reporting on the band's appearance at the Whisky-a-Go-Go in 1977, *Variety* magazine said, "AC/DC are from Australia, where there is apparently a reasonably thriving punk scene. Certainly the attitude is consistent with the popular image of gruff cowboy types from Down Under." It was a cursory summary that said nothing about the music aside from its country of origin.

Variety is a trade magazine for the entertainment industry, so their superficial and uninformed take, in retrospect, is somewhat excusable; *Rolling Stone*'s disdain for AC/DC over the years is not. Unlike the powers that be at the magazine who ignored and cursorily reported on the band from 1976 on, senior writer David Fricke at least understood why AC/DC worked. In his review of *Back in Black* in 1980, he wrote, "*Back in Black* is not only the best of AC/DC's six American albums, it's the apex of heavy metal art: the first LP since *Led Zeppelin II* that captures all the blood, sweat and arrogance of the genre . . . While Malcolm Young anchors such songs as 'Hell's Bells,' 'What Do You Do For Money Honey?' and 'Shake a Leg,' . . . with his hamfisted, almost percussive rhythm guitar playing, brother Angus runs riotously up and down the neck of his axe, peeling off banzai solos that are the studio equivalents of his notorious schoolboy tantrums onstage. Since less is often more in AC/DC's warlike world, the only luxury the group allows itself is a clean, invigorating production job by Robert John Lange. Unfortunately, a lot of people can't recognize the talent because of the noise. AC/DC may not be everybody's cup of joy, but they're not rock-and-roll's village idiots either."

Fricke, who remains a bastion of quality at a magazine that has seen better days, was in the minority even back then. Historically *Rolling Stone* is an institution; for years it was the preeminent American forum for music criticism, a leader that influenced the opinions of critics in mainstream periodicals across the land. The magazine's grudging acceptance of AC/DC surely went a long way to leading virtually every other general-interest pop culture and current events publication to take the same approach. More or less across the board, the mainstream media's relationship with the band has been one of forced acceptance when they've been acknowledged at all. In AC/DC's thirty-five-year history, the band has graced the cover of *Rolling Stone* exactly twice—once in 1980, when *Back in Black* was the bestselling album in the land, and again in 2008, when *Black Ice* was the bestselling album in the land. There was no Bon Scott memorial issue, no exclusive "in the studio" pieces (an honor that far too many lesser bands, from Creed to No Doubt, can claim), and no fitting recognition of AC/DC's musical contribution to rock and roll in any of *Rolling Stone*'s endless "greatest" lists. "Literally the last story we did on AC/DC that was of any size was in 1980," *Rolling Stone* music editor Jason Fine told the Associated Press in 2008. "We had literally not covered the band at all. We did very few short news stories and *Rolling Stone* was not the only one. AC/DC was never a band that was really covered a lot by the critics, they were always kind of looked down on."

Not every single media outlet has ignored AC/DC, of course. The playing-oriented and exclusively hard rock and metal magazines have always given them praise, from *Guitar World* and *Guitar Player* to *Metal Hammer* and *Kerrang!*. It's no surprise that these publications, focused on the art of playing and the world of metal and hard rock, would understand AC/DC. But it is surprising that magazines devoted to upholding and documenting the history of rock and roll would not. The mainstream has always lumped AC/DC in with heavy metal, which, if anything, is undeniable proof that they just don't get it. As David Fricke said in 1980, it seems that, through the years, most critics have been unable to see the talent through the noise. That noise also seems to be why AC/DC is generally regarded by critics as a heavy metal rather than a classic hard rock band, a label that segregates them from the well of music deemed worthy of analysis by the esteemed music press.

Heavy metal features some of the most proficient, technically sound playing in any brand of rock music, but the extreme nature of the music will always keep it outside of and underappreciated by the mainstream press. AC/DC was never that brand of band, however; they only share heavy metal's extremity in volume and intensity. Their playing, songwriting, and image have always been true to the roots of straight-ahead rock and roll. Critics more than anyone should have seen that, particularly those who had watched the evolution of rock from Chuck Berry through his '60s disciples—the Stones, the Who, Led Zeppelin—into the large-scale, arena-size rock of the early '70s. Those critical voices, whose opinions mattered more then than they do today, for the most part seemed confused by AC/DC, and time did nothing to change that. Generally they seemed unable to distinguish the band's blues roots and rock-and-roll boogie from the more complicated constructions and jackhammer tempos of such '70s acts as Iron Maiden and Judas Priest. "I never understood why anyone called AC/DC metal," says Slayer's Kerry King. "They're a hard rock band, without a doubt. I think they're the most popular bar band ever. I would never consider them metal. They are the blueprint for fucking rock and roll."

In contrast, the foreign press (excluding Australia, where it goes without saying they always understood their local heroes) seemed to get what AC/DC was doing. In the UK in the late '70s, as punk rock was displacing glam rock, AC/DC found fans both in print and in the clubs. *Melody Maker*'s review of *Powerage* in 1976 wasn't deeply analytical, but it got right to the point: "One listen to *Powerage*, their fourth album, and you just know they mean it . . . There's not much to be said about these Aussie rockers that hasn't been said before, although I'll be the first to admit after this album that the weight of their rock and roll force was previously understated . . . An album I'd unreservedly recommend to any fan of unpretentious grass-roots hard rock, and certainly the best I've heard of that ilk in some considerable time."

Truthfully, even as AC/DC's sales surpassed those of just about every single rock band of note and most pop acts of modern times, not much changed in the way they were analyzed and discussed in the music press. Even in 2008, as the print media lined up to praise *Black Ice* as AC/DC's greatest album since *Back in Black,* it was obvious that many of the editors at those outlets were either conflicted or just confused about having to do so. A review of the press surrounding the album reads like an exercise in mixed messages and grudging praise: most of the pieces, even those in musically savvy publications, lacked enthusiasm and seemed to be necessitated by commerce. Nowhere was this love-hate confusion more apparent than in the *New York Times.* The paper ran a lengthy interview with the band in October 2008, conducted by Rob Levine, that, in a neutral, journalistic manner, got to the bottom of the band's enduring appeal. "Gradually, and without getting much media attention, AC/DC has become the most popular currently active rock band in the country, to judge by albums sold . . . AC/DC's commercial success flies in the face of conventional music industry wisdom . . . AC/DC gets less attention than many bands it outsells. Its songs receive less airplay than those of Aerosmith, according to Neilsen Broadcast Data Systems. Its members get less attention in the gossip columns than the children of the Beatles. And it's never been a critical favorite. The band makes no pretense to art and its lyrics often contain what might be called single entendres. For this and much else, Angus is unapologetic. 'People say it's juvenile music but pardon me . . . I thought rock and roll was supposed to be juvenile. You sing what you know. What am I going to write about, Rembrandt?' "

This very fair-minded portrait was followed a month later by a live review of the band's show at Madison Square

Garden by Jon Caramanica that was so decidedly slanted that it read like a self-appointed critic's blog or teenager's journal. Caramanica, a journalist who primarily writes about hip-hop, is either unqualified to judge rock-and-roll musicianship or he simply chose to separate himself from the media crowd by being the only critic in any major publication to find such gross fault with the band's live show. That fault, it should be noted, was primarily of a philosophical and visual nature. "All the recent talk of how AC/DC is due for critical reprisal? Ignore it. That secret history in which this committedly low-brow 35-year-old band is actually one of the most influential hard-rock groups ever to have graced an arena stage? Dubious at best." In describing the show, he said that the pyrotechnics and effects were "glorious in the way most uncomplicated pleasures are" and that, apart from "slightly peppier bass on 'Dirty Deeds Done Dirt Cheap'" and "a minor drum shift on 'Thunderstruck,'" "the show had the visual charm and poetry of a construction site." It's interesting that Caramanica, a fan of rhythm-based music, missed what music appreciators such as Rick Rubin have always understood: AC/DC are masters of the groove. They have worked an undeniably essential, primal human beat into the ground for three decades. That backbeat—and to a large degree that subject matter—are no different from those of hip-hop, a genre where outlaw behavior, arrogance, humor, and sexual exploit reign supreme. In that light, Caramanica's biased, inch-deep review was at least downright entertaining in its shortsightedness; it was proof once again that many music critics feel more comfortable arguing the merits of Auto Tune and T Pain than they do the harmonies of Buddy Holly and the solos of Buddy Guy. Some things are just easier to identify and describe.

For the most part, however, the critical opinion of *Black Ice* and AC/DC in 2008 was that the band that had never been creative enough to change their formula and experiment musically was suddenly a team of musical geniuses for having never changed their tune. Accolades were rained down on them at every turn: they were inducted into the Rock and Roll Hall of Fame by Steven Tyler and given lead record reviews in magazines that weren't even around when *Back in Black* came out. Of course, the band couldn't have cared less about any of it. "The critics have always been a little flippant with AC/DC," Brian Johnson told the Associated Press in 2008, "and it's always easy to have a quick little joke or a dig at the expense of it, the easy riffs, . . . and they're all dead wrong. The easiest riffs in the world are the hardest ones to write because they are very few. 'Highway to Hell' is easy, but you ask a guitarist, it's not that easy. Nobody can write them because easy things are difficult to write . . . and to put them together in different computations and to come up with something fresh and different. It's genius, but the critics never figure that out."

The truth, in my opinion at least, is that *Black Ice* isn't even close to *Back in Black* and will never be a classic on a par with most of the band's catalog. The album has its moments, and overall it is a satisfying listen, but it did not deserve the attention it got. The band, however, did, which is why the unanimous praise was awkward. It was a clear case of critics realizing that there were magazines and newspapers to be sold and Internet hits to be had on the back of a band they'd ignored even in the face of staggering album sales and tour revenues over the years. Elvis Costello once explained his critical acclaim by saying that music critics like bands that look the way *they* do, and I couldn't agree more. I've also never seen a band that looks less like a pack of music critics than AC/DC, unless there is a music magazine staffed by former roadies for Deep Purple that I'm unaware of. Whatever it was, in 2008, critics found something to latch onto in AC/DC that they'd somehow never found before. The music and the players had not changed, and if anything only the times were more different than ever. Regardless, it made as little sense that the media embraced the band in 2008 of all times as it did that they'd rejected or ignored them all along. Then again, AC/DC is a recession-proof band.

"The foundation of AC/DC's music is broad strokes," J3 says, "and when broad strokes are done well, they are very powerful. That beat, which is driven by Malcolm Young's guitar playing, is so primal and so simplified that you either get it or you don't. I think that's the thing that all the critics have been missing, because they usually just call AC/DC dumb. Regardless of what they think of the lyrics, they typically say that the music is simple, easy, derivative—which means *dumb*. It is the same thing you read when a critic doesn't understand hip-hop: they say it's not music because it's a guy talking over a repetitive beat. Whatever. You can pooh-pooh that all you want in your magazine, but that dumb beat, whether it's rock or rap, makes people dance. It's what people react to. AC/DC has that primal beat. They embody that simple nature of what rock and roll truly is."

Regardless of how *Black Ice* stands up to the rest of the AC/DC catalog, the band's tour was, as usual, a showcase of the unquestionable fortitude of their legacy. J3 is correct: simplicity done right is much more powerful than complexity—particularly at high volume. Malcolm Young's expertly timed rhythm playing sounded, as it always has, absolutely huge. It was full of clarity, where something busy at that volume would have been nothing but noise. Regardless of what any backseat driver says, too many musicians agree that what AC/DC does musically isn't easy: it's a precise art that leaves no room for error. At a time when the pop culture moment is all that matters, to see a group of retirement-age musicians play two hours of jaw-droppingly powerful technologically unassisted rock and roll culled from thirty years of expertly crafted songs is a greater testament to their merit than anything I can write right here.

Whether you see them on video or see them in concert, see AC/DC live—as soon as you can. There really is nothing like it. It's uncompromised, pure adrenaline and it doesn't get any better. "At the end of the day, AC/DC is a blues-based hard rock-and-roll band that comes from the trenches," Slash says. "They're a glorified bar band. Sure, they've gotten huge and they've gotten older, but they've never really tried to operate as anything other than that, which is why people love them—and also why people hate them. Everything about the way they've survived and how they've stuck to their guns all these years means a lot to me. They were one of my idols growing up and they still are today. To me, AC/DC are exactly how a rock band should be—how simple it all should be and how good you can do it if you give it your all. I saw them this past year and they were still just *so good* live. The show was everything you'd want it to be: too loud and just fucking insane. It reminded me of why I do what I do. That one show made me feel seventeen again."

CHAPTER FIVE

YOU GOT THE LUST

I DON'T CARE HOW PERSONAL

the nature of the art form may be, a performance cannot exist in a vacuum. No performers play for themselves alone (though one might argue the case when it comes to mimes), because the essence of performance isn't just communication, it is *connection*. There are few human stories that haven't already been told and there are no human emotions that haven't been felt before in our two hundred thousand years on Earth. Art and performance are creative retellings of our communal history, meant to be witnessed and consumed by an audience; without a witness, a performance is practice and it has no meaning beyond the player's experience. Performance can be understood via the age-old adage about the tree falling in the woods: if no one sees it, does it make a sound? If the tree is a tree, yes it does, but if the tree is a band? I say, unequivocally, no, it does not. But if you turn your amps up to eleven and play the show of your lives in a cornfield to no one, only you and your bandmates have the right to care about it; but if you play to a crowd of twenty in a dive bar and kill it nonetheless, you're laying the pipes of legend. Without fans, a rock band might as well try to make history in their parents' garage, because without fans a rock band is nothing.

"I have liked AC/DC since I was a kid," says John Gaffney, a forty-one-year-old fan from Brooklyn, New York. "I've always been into heavy, old school rock. I saw Metallica at L'amour, which is a legendary metal club, back before their first album even came out. AC/DC I love for their lyrics, the overall heaviness of the music, and the tightness of the band. Live, they are one of the tightest bands I've ever seen. They're amazing performers. And you can put on an AC/DC song from twenty years ago and it still holds its own against any rock from today. It's just as hard and together as anything new."

Winning fans is one thing, and keeping them is another, but inspiring ludicrous devotion is something else entirely. Particularly today, when popular culture and technology feed our insatiable interests with an overabundance of input, committing to one band without fail through the thick and thin—for *years*—is the exception, not the norm. The music is what draws us in, but it takes more than great tunes to keep fans coming back year after year. This is something that younger, of-the-moment rock acts are sure to discover in the near future. Internet hits and MySpace friends seem like powerful stats in today's music industry, but what will any of that mean in a few years when those friends don't have as much time and disposable income to waste? The nuts and bolts, or dollars and cents, of a band's relationship with their fans are the only things that translate into tangible longevity. Fans are a band's sponsors; it is their hard-earned dollars that keep artists afloat through ticket, CD, and merchandise purchases. To justify this expense over the long run, fans must continue to believe in them. A band's image and attitude play a major role in this ongoing relationship with their audience, and their every artistic decision affects this symbiosis at all levels. Whether the image they project is as otherworldly as David Bowie's, as demonic as Marilyn Manson's, as wizardly as Led Zeppelin's, or as rakish as the Rolling Stones'; that image speaks as powerfully to the fans as the music does. A band's image sends a message that must communicate with the audience as clearly and definitively as the music itself. The combination of the two is the meat and potatoes that nurtures the fan base.

AC/DC's relationship with their public has always been one of direct supply and demand between producer and consumer. They've always kept their private lives separate from the band and allowed their onstage personae to speak for them—but theirs has never been a case of using artifice to sell. They've put forth the same image from the time they first graced a barroom floor to the last stadium they played. AC/DC came from the trenches and they've never changed their behavior or their relationship with those who support them. AC/DC's success, for better or for worse, made hair metal more legitimate in the '80s, but it did not establish the hierarchy between the bands and their fans that grew up around that genre. Late '80s metal bands, from Poison, Cinderella, and Whitesnake to Def Leppard and Bon Jovi, flaunted an image that set them apart from their audience. From their videos to the subjects of their songs, those acts depicted an extra special existence, one filled with girls and booze and drugs and jets, that every man could aspire to but only the guys in the band could call their own.

Though they've never been associated with it, AC/DC actually represented the values of the grunge era that displaced hair metal more than hair metal itself. Bands like Nirvana and Pearl Jam grew in popularity in the '90s because they wrote songs that their fans could relate to, and also because, onstage and off, they looked no different from them. Grunge bands eschewed rock star pomp and circumstance, and this was seen as something revolutionary by the media and the masses at the time. Identifying with your audience to that degree is completely admirable—but it's something AC/DC has been doing since 1973.

AC/DC may travel first class these days, but image-wise, they still carry themselves as glamorously as they did on their first bare-bones, no-clean-clothes cross-continent tour of Australia. The members of the band all have multiple homes and spend their spare time engaging in elite leisure activities such as car racing (Brian Johnson) and still-life painting (Angus Young) that the average Joe has little time for, but considering the excesses expected of international music icons, the members of AC/DC are downright thrifty. It is consistent with the band's evolution, which has never strayed far from their core values: the stages have gotten bigger over time, but their egos have not—none of which has gone unnoticed by the band's audience. AC/DC's dedication to doing what they set out to do, despite the times, despite the odds, and despite the critics, has unequivocally earned them a three-decade-thick mob of fans as diehard as their riffs.

"When I was in junior high in 1979," Rick Rubin told *Rolling Stone* in 2004, "my classmates all liked Led Zeppelin but I loved AC/DC. I got turned on to them when I heard them play 'Problem Child' on [weekly TV show] *The Midnight Special*. Like Led Zeppelin, they were rooted in American R & B, but AC/DC took it to a minimal extreme that I had never heard before. Of course I didn't know that back then. I only knew that they sounded better than any other band . . . I first saw them play in 1979, before their singer Bon Scott died and was replaced by Brian Johnson. They were opening for Ted Nugent at Madison Square Garden. The crowd yanked all the chairs off the floor and piled them into a pyramid in front of the stage. It was a tribute to how great they were."

AC/DC's fans have always embodied—and actively demonstrated—their dedication to the band to an extent that other groups only dream of. Whether it means driving nearly a thousand miles in twenty hours to buy tickets, as one Australian fan did this past year, or flying around the world to catch the first show of a tour, AC/DC fans are among rock's most dedicated. Rock-and-roll devotion is often steeped in nostalgia, as people typically revere the bands from their teen years. But once those years fade away, so does a good majority of those fans who simply lose interest. Not so with AC/DC, whose fans are a lot like soccer fanatics: they're in it for life, even through losing seasons. And they have to be, considering the gaps between albums and tours with only memories and the back catalog to keep their faith alive.

"I don't think being in a band means you stop becoming a fan of the music that got you there," says Kerry King of Slayer. "I'm in Slayer and I'm a fan of Slayer. I'm a fan of AC/DC, and that's never changed, because they've stayed true to their sound. I'm still a huge Judas Priest fan, but after they put out *Point of Entry* and after that *Turbo*, I lost some respect for them. I remember the first time I saw them live, which was around *Point of Entry*, Rob Halford was wearing denim after I'd seen nothing but pictures of him wearing leather. Visually that was something that didn't relate to everything I'd known of them, and it changed the way I saw them forever. I'm still a fan, but I don't hold them to as high a standard, because I see them as a band who might throw me a curve ball at any time. AC/DC was never like that. And they never will be."

The greatest thing about AC/DC's what-you-see-is-what-you-get legacy is that they appeal to younger fans despite the band members' age and inaccessibility (relative to today's Twitterly standards). While most rock bands hover at the end of a mouse click, AC/DC is still behind a decades-old firewall. It hasn't seemed to hurt them any.

"I remember seeing AC/DC back in 2000, and what struck me the most was the age group of the fans," says Sevendust/Tommy Lee guitarist J3. "There were lots of mommies bringing their sons and daughters and I really didn't expect that. It was a New York show and it was as sold out as possible, and as people left Madison Square Garden it reminded me of the movie *The Warriors*. They were like gangs being let loose on the streets of New York. People were riled up out of their minds, singing the songs at the top of their lungs, pouring out into the streets, all going to a bar—it was just *on*. I hadn't felt that kind of energy since I saw Van Halen in 1984, when people were blowing shit up in the parking lot at the Meadowlands in New Jersey. That's what it was like at big rock concerts in the eighties, but AC/DC's concerts are *still* like that. It doesn't matter if the people in the crowd are forty-five years old now, they're still going berserk. And they don't care that they have to go to work tomorrow."

"AC/DC isn't like any other band touring right now," Tommy Lee agrees. "Here's why I say this. I fucking love those guys, and I have my reasons, but they're the only band I can name that my two sons actually came to *me* about. I hadn't even heard about their tour dates until my little guys came into my room and said, 'Hey, Dad, AC/DC is coming here, do you know about this?' I was like, 'Uh . . . no, dudes, I don't, what's the deal?' 'AC/DC are coming, can we go with you? Do you know those guys? We love those guys!' It was awesome. I encourage my sons musically however they want, and I'd take them to see any band they want to see, but fuck, was I glad to hear that AC/DC was who they really wanted to see. It was just so cool, and we went together and it was good times. My youngest son is playing guitar and cello now, and I couldn't imagine a better visual lesson than taking him to watch Angus and Malcolm do their thing."

. . .

If there is no better form of flattery than imitation, AC/DC's fans are a flattering bunch. A cursory perusal of the Internet turns up a rich fan-web and an extensive international network of cover bands. As any bar owner will tell you, a cover band is only as good as the audience they draw, which is why most working cover groups opt to play a wide variety of popular songs rather than specialize in the work of just one group. But AC/DC cover bands, providing they're skilled enough, never hurt for work or for crowds. They bridge the gap between the band's music and the fans' devotion, because no good cover act can play the role if they're not fans first. As a fan who missed AC/DC during the eight years preceding *Black Ice*, I've seen my share of tribute bands to get my fix. There are many capable, nationally known acts, but in my opinion—aside from the now-defunct Dirty Deeds out of Santa Barbara, California—Bonfire, a tribute to Bon Scott—era AC/DC out of Los Angeles, is the best I've ever seen.

Bonfire have been at it for eight years so far, and from their outfits to their playing, their accuracy is exacting. Some of the members came from other tribute bands, but most of them were musicians just looking to supplement their income and keep up their skills. None of them expected to be as excited about the enterprise as they still are. "I was concerned when I joined that I'd get tired of playing the music," says Forrest, the drummer. "But it just gets more and more fun to play. The music is timeless and I appreciate it to no end as we keep digging deeper into the catalog and extending our repertoire. There's really not a bad song in the bunch. Nobody else has been able to do what AC/DC has done with those three fundamental rock-and-roll chords. It's something you can't explain."

Playing AC/DC songs well is one thing, but play-acting AC/DC is a responsibility the band members don't take lightly, particularly Sean, who fronts the band as Bon. From his curly locks to his nimble voice, he is every inch a fitting tribute. It's something he takes great pride in because he realizes that every time he takes to the stage, whether in front of fifty people at a local bar or fifteen thousand at an outdoor festival, he is the embodiment of a powerful icon. "AC/DC fans are the greatest fans in the world," he says. "They love AC/DC so much that they push all of that love on to us when they come to our shows. They appreciate us keeping the music alive; they'll come up and hug us and cry and be so thankful that we're doing what we do that we have no choice but to want to do it better. What started out as, 'Sure, I'll try singing in a tribute band,' has gone, for me, to feeling like we are conserving a very precious link between people and the band. It's an honor to do that."

Ultimately, AC/DC's fans are the greatest because their band is the greatest. The Youngs and Co. founded an outfit dedicated to the primal, tribal, simple, unrelenting beat of early rock and roll. From Chuck Berry to Elvis, they tuned in, absorbed the fundamentals, and made their music a single-minded lifelong tribute to that sound. They crafted something defiantly outside of their time, honed it to a razor-sharp edge, and never strayed. It should be no surprise to anyone who understands the nature of dedication that AC/DC's fans are with them come hell or high water. "The thing about AC/DC isn't that they invented anything new," Slash says. "They were lifting licks just like every blues-based rock band has done since Chuck Berry. What they did differently than anyone else at the time when they came out was do it without any pretense, without any bullshit—without anything dishonest. AC/DC has always been one hundred percent genuine. That had as tremendous an influence on me as the music did. They have a synergy that can never be replicated and they've always been themselves. They've cornered the market, as far as I'm concerned. Why would I listen to anyone else when I want to get that vibe? Other bands can try, but no one can do it better."

ON OCTOBER 26, 2008,

I was one of the lucky three thousand fans who saw AC/DC's final dress rehearsal of the Rock 'N Roll Train tour at the Wachovia Arena in Wilkes-Barre, Pennsylvania. The band was excited, in top form, and played with all the tremendous energy they had when I saw them twice more on that leg. I learned from someone in their camp that they'd run through a good number of older songs during their rehearsals that week—many of which, like "Shoot to Thrill" and "Bad Boy Boogie," I would have loved to have seen. Even without those, the show was fantastic, if too brief, but well worth the wait. My seat that night was about ten rows back on Malcolm's side, and it was the closest I'd ever been to the stage. And as if seeing them up close after an eight-year hiatus wasn't thrilling enough, being that near to the pyro and props in an arena at a fraction of its capacity was what I imagine it would have been like standing in a doorway next to André the Giant.

The music and the return of the band were momentous enough, but that night I realized once again that AC/DC have the most dedicated, committed (and worthy of being committed) fans in all of rock and roll. In the parking lot I met two who had flown all the way from Perth to see the show: they'd traveled over thirty-two hours in two days, spent their monthly wages on airfare, and thought nothing of turning right around the morning after and heading back. They'd bought the tickets from someone who had won them on the radio and, from what it sounded like, made their arrangements without really consulting with their employers. They were entirely unconcerned with losing their jobs (one worked as an electrician, the other as a bartender) or falling asleep on the clock upon their return, since the bartender of the pair planned to head into work hours after they landed. No, their greatest concern when I ran into them was how to get properly amped up for showtime. "We've had a steady stream of lager to get us through all the travel," one of them, named John, said. "I think I need to switch to Red Bull. Those girls over there just gave me a few shots of Jack and I'm slagging, mate."

He looked over at his friend. "You think I might be jet-lagged?" he asked and flashed a toothy grin.

"I don't care if you are," said his friend. "All you need is more beer, mate. Red Bull is for little boys."

I told them that, though I understood how special the occasion was, I had to wonder what possessed them to spend all their money and risk their jobs to make the trip, when AC/DC was certain to play their hometown later on in the year. I mentioned that the same amount of money, probably less, could easily buy them front-row seats to that gig.

John looked at me like I was insane. "You ever been to Perth, mate?"

"I've been to Australia, but no, I didn't make it out there," I said.

A mild look of disdain came over his face. "Well you do know who's buried there, don't you?"

"Oh yeah—of course! The infamous Ronald Belford Scott," I said.

"We've got Bon's grave there, we've got a statue of him in our town. You think AC/DC fans with all that in their backyard aren't going to the ends of the earth if they get the chance to see something like this?"

"Yeah, but that's not even it," his friend interrupted. "The band's not coming to Perth for months. We see this show and it's miles of bragging rights for us back home, mate!"

Across the parking lot, crowds were gathered in the freezing cold swapping stories, drinking, and otherwise just rocking out to the nearest stereo blasting AC/DC. There were many Anguses in full, custom-made schoolboy suits, many Brian Johnson caps, and many, many women straight out of AC/DC's lyrical world.

"This is a once-in-a-lifetime opportunity," said Shelby, a blond, tan, sexy twentysomething from Boca Raton, Florida. "My whole family are AC/DC fans. They're so jealous I'm here!"

"Were you worried that the band wasn't going to come back after being away for so long?" I asked.

"No way! *Stiff Upper Lip* was so great and that tour was so awesome that I knew they'd come back," she said. "They just took their time. They have their formula down so well, why not? At this point they're like a machine. Like a slot machine! You just have to put quarters in. I mean, if the Stones can do it and they're, like, sixty-five, AC/DC can keep touring. They put on a better show anyway. I saw the Stones last tour and they sound great, but I was bored."

Fans had come from all over the country, and some of them, like Danny, a drummer and mechanic's assistant from Bakersfield, California, had made it an epic journey. He and four friends used the show as an opportunity to drive cross-country, crashing with friends all along the route.

"I'd go anywhere to see this fucking band," he said. "I've been waiting eight years for this. I knew it was coming so I saved my money and quit my fucking job to be here. All of us are starting a band together when we get back, so we're in this shit together, man!"

"This is like our trip to the fucking motherland of rock," said Nate, the unnamed band's bass player.

"Have you guys all played together yet?" I asked.

"Not yet," Danny said. "But we've been planning what it's going to sound like. We've had lots of hours on the road."

"What's it going to sound like?" I asked.

"Heavy metal."

"Awesome. Like what era? Or which bands?"

"Just heavy metal, man," Nate said. "Classic heavy metal. AC/DC, Scorpions, just good heavy metal."

"Have you thought of a name?" I asked.

"Well, AC/DC is taken!" Danny said.

"So is Iron Maiden!" Nate said. "We'll work that out on the trip home. We're all gonna get inspired by the best band in the world in just a little while."

"Why is AC/DC the best rock-and-roll band in the world?" I asked them.

"Oh, man," Danny said. "They have the best tunes. Angus and Malcolm are fucking amazing. Best riffs ever written in rock and roll. And they're still doing it and doing it well at their age."

"Yeah," Nate said. "And they've stayed honest. They're a huge band that's known outside of heavy metal. And they're the only band like that who never turned gay. Aerosmith? They write, like, Barbra Streisand songs that my mom likes. Metallica? They cut their hair and turned gay. AC/DC never did any of that. AC/DC are still fucking cool."

On my way into the arena I was on line behind Lois and Chet Bailey, who had come from upstate New York. Lois had been seeing the band regularly since she was a teenager and was now taking her son to his first show. "I'm starting him off right," she said. "I first saw AC/DC in 1979, and he's seeing them in 2009. It's like passing on a gift from his mom."

"Is AC/DC your favorite band?" I asked her son.

"Oh yeah," he said. "Angus is so awesome. I like new bands, too, like Mastadon—they're really good. But I really like AC/DC and Led Zeppelin and stuff. Those bands started it all."

That night, and every time I've seen AC/DC, I've always been happy to note the steady number of teenage—and younger—fans at their shows. At a time when technologies such as Auto Tune and triggered drum samples (not to mention guitar techs playing parts offstage for bands both young and old) have enabled players with less than professional talent to come off like prodigies both in the studio and in concert, it's reassuring to see that some of the kids are no fools. I don't care what anyone says—there is no substitute for blood-sweat-and-tears playing because it simply can't be faked. Whatever the cause, whether it's the advent of *Guitar Hero* and *Rock Band* or the rise of a generation with less of an us-versus-them attitude toward their parents' music, younger and younger music fans are embracing classic rock. The technology that enables someone like Fall Out Boy to replicate the stadium-sized sound of Queen or Aerosmith (without the skill) did not exist back when those bands' classic records were recorded. Great, timeless classic rock artists relied on talent, and that is one thing that no machine can mimic—the individuality of humanity.

I for one am not surprised that AC/DC continues to be a lightning rod for younger rock fans. Unlike other artists considered founding fathers of the genre, AC/DC does not sound dated. They sound precisely the way they did in 1973: out of time, masters of their own universe, and a force to be reckoned with. They are older now but their music knows no age. It will make them immortal after they've hung it up and gone back to their lives away from the legacy. In that cold parking lot in rural Pennsylvania, the lucky three

thousand of us knew that. We were not there to be enter-
tained. We were there to bear witness, to take part in one
moment in a long, storied history. We were there to fire our
guns, to give back to those who had given to us. We were
there to pay tribute to a band that ends every show with a
salute and a reminder that they know what is important,
that they know what matters—and that they know just why
we're there.

ACKNOWLEDGMENTS

I'd like to thank Lisa Gallagher, who knew immediately why this book had to be written. Though she is no longer at the company publishing this book, her spirit is alive and well within these pages. Lynn Grady, who oversaw the editing and production of the book from concept to completion, was an incredibly enthusiastic and essential accomplice. Lynn's devotion to making this a success is as amplified and all-out as the band itself and I'm lucky to have her on my side, as any writer would be. I'd like to thank Katie Field for her research and assistance. I'd also like to thank my intrepid assistant, Paige Plum, for keeping me organized. One of the greatest allies I have in the world of publishing is Todd Gallopo, who designed the cover and interior pages. I've worked with Todd on as many of my projects as possible since 2002, and I'm happy to say that we're both good friends and coworkers. As a person, as a designer, and as an overall aesthetic presence in the art of publishing, he and his partner in design (and life), Andrea, are people I'm lucky to know. Their team is now a part of Igniter, my publishing company with Neil Strauss, and I couldn't be happier. I'd like to thank all of my friends, especially Jason Catlin, Shawn Dailey, John Allen III, and the rest of you who sat and talked AC/DC with me: your insights fueled my bonfire. Thanks to professors Stone and Stewart, to Slash, to Tommy Lee, and to Kerry King for their time. Not first but definitely foremost, thank you, Shane—this book is for *you*. Without you I'd never have known true happiness or gone the extra mile on this or anything else I've done since the day we met. Floyd, thank you for your companionship and patience, and for knowing that barking is entirely overrated. Lastly yet hardly leastly, thank you AC/DC for giving it your all for thirty-five years and counting. And when you weren't doing that, thank you for staying the hell out of the limelight and letting the music do the talking. Bon Scott, R.I.P.

BIBLIOGRAPHY

BOOKS

Bunton, Richard. *AC/DC: Hell Ain't a Bad Place to Be* (London: Omnibus Press, 1983).

Dome, Malcolm. *AC/DC: The Definitive History* (London: Virgin Publishing, 2002).

Engleheart, Murray, and Arnaud Duriex. *AC/DC, Maximum Rock & Roll: The Ultimate Story of the World's Greatest Rock and Roll Band* (Sydney: HarperCollins Australia, 2006).

Huxley, Martin. *AC/DC: The World's Heaviest Rock* (New York: St. Martin's Press, 2003).

Stenning, Paul. *AC/DC: Two Sides to Every Glory: The Complete Biography* (New Malden, England: Chrome Dreams, 2007).

Walker, Clinton. *Highway to Hell: The Life and Death of AC/DC Legend Bon Scott* (Portland, OR: Verse Chorus Press, 2007).

PERIODICALS

Altman, Billy. "AC/DC, *High Voltage,* review." *Rolling Stone,* December 16, 1976.

Associated Press. "AC/DC May Finally Get a Little Respect," November 6, 2008.

Caramanica, Jon. "Rock of a Certain Age, Complete with Inflatable Doll." *New York Times,* November 13, 2008.

Doherty, Harry. "AC/DC, *Powerage,* review." *Melody Maker,* June 3, 1978.

Donovan, Patrick. "Lewd, Loud, and Very, Very Big." *Sunday Age* (Melbourne, Australia), October 8, 2000.

Doyle, Tom. "Is This Any Way for a 53-Year-Old Man to Behave?" *Q Magazine,* November 2008.

Editors, Todd. "AC/DC, 5 Songs, Whisky, L.A." *Variety,* October 12, 1977.

Eliezer, Christie. "AC/DC Tour Sparks Excitement Down Under." *Billboard,* August 31, 1996.

Everly, Dave. "AC/DC, *Black Ice,* review." *Q Magazine,* November 2008.

Fontaine, Angus. "Rock of Ages: AC/DC Playing Bigger and Louder Than Ever." *Daily Telegraph* (Sydney, Australia), October 28, 2000.

Fricke, David. "AC/DC and the Gospel of Rock and Roll." *Rolling Stone,* November 2008.

———. "AC/DC, *Back in Black,* review." *Rolling Stone,* November 27, 1980.

Gett, Steve. "AC/DC Go to Hell." *Melody Maker,* November 10, 1979.

Kaplan, Ira. "AC/DC's High-Voltage Sonic Assault." *Rolling Stone,* November 16, 1978.

Levine, Robert. "Ageless and Defiant, AC/DC Stays On

Top Without Going Digital." *New York Times,* October 10, 2008.

Price, Matt. "Long Time at the Top but AC/DC Still Rock On." *Weekend Australian,* January 20, 2001.

Sunday Herald Sun (Melbourne, Australia), "AC/DC Not Game to Mime," October 22, 2000.

Sydney Morning Herald (Australia), "Acca Dacca and 17 Vans to Shake Us This Summer," October 3, 2000.

Tulich, Katherine. "AC/DC Still Turned On." *Sunday Mail* (Queensland, Australia), October 29, 2000.

BJOERN KOMMERELL

Anthony Bozza is the author of four *New York Times* bestsellers, including *Whatever You Say I Am: The Life and Times of Eminem; Slash*, cowritten with Slash; and the number one bestselling *Too Fat to Fish*, cowritten with Artie Lange. Bozza was a staff writer and editor for *Rolling Stone* magazine for seven years, during which he profiled a diverse range of artists from Eminem and the Wu-Tang Clan to Trent Reznor and U2. He lives in New York City and on the Web at www.anthonybozza.net.

11-06-09